Graham Winter

Graham Winter is a psychologist specialising in the field of performance enhancement with sporting and business clients.

In the sport area his appointments have included Psychologist to the 1988 Australian Olympic Team in Seoul and Co-ordinator of Sport Psychology for the 1992 Olympic team in Barcelona. He consults to the Australian Institute of Sport and manages the Sport Psychology unit at the South Australian Sports Institute. His clients have included world champions in cycling, shooting, lacrosse, archery and trampolining.

In business, he has managed the Human Resources Division of Touche Ross Services and worked as a senior consultant with Coopers and Lybrand. He is regularly involved in consulting to business organisations on the applications of performance psychology.

Graham also has a successful sporting background, having been a member of Sheffield Shield and McDonalds Cup winning cricket teams in 1982 and 1984, respectively. He is the author of *The Psychology of Cricket*.

Christopher Hamilton

Christopher Hamilton has over a decade's experience as a consultant in the areas of organisation development, performance management, strategic and long-range planning and psychological assessment. Prior to this, Chris was engaged in university teaching and research after taking graduate studies in education and psychology

Formerly a consultant with WD Scott Australia, Chris is now a national Director of Davidson Trahaire, a leading organisation consulting company with offices throughout Australia and with international affiliations. His company's clients have included many multi-nationals in most market sectors including transport, banking, food processing, computing, petrochemical, mining, professional services and aerospace. The company has consulted to more than half of Australia's largest corporations and institutions.

Chris has addressed world conferences in North America and Asia on the topics of high potential and high achievement individuals and teams. In addition, this work has taken him to Europe and South America.

THE BUSINESS Athlete

WINNING THE INNER GAME OF BUSINESS

GRAHAM WINTER AND CHRISTOPHER HAMILTON

SUN
AUSTRALIA

To the memory of our parents

&

To Carol, Mark and Ben

First published 1992 by Pan Macmillan Publishers Australia
a division of Pan Macmillan Australia Pty Limited
63-71 Balfour Street, Chippendale, Sydney
A.C.N. 001 184 014

National Library of Australia
cataloguing-in-publication data:

Winter, Graham.
The business athlete.

ISBN 0 7251 0708 1.

1. Success in business—Psychological aspects. 2.
Psychology, Industrial. I. Hamilton, Christopher J.
II. Title.

650.1

Typeset in 10/11 pt Andover by Midland Typesetters
Printed in Australia by The Book Printer

FOREWORD

There is much about the athlete that is relevant to business. The athlete knows that to win he or she has to excel and beat the competition. To be successful requires dedication, knowing what level of performance will be required, setting a target, and developing a personal plan to achieve that target by a specified day. The same is true of those in business who want to succeed.

In sport, Australians understand that athletes cannot win gold medals, Test matches or Grand Slam events unless they are internationally competitive. To succeed you have to be the best, measured in international terms. Australians also know that yesterday's standards are not good enough to win today's events. Athletes are continually improving and doing better than their predecessors. A sprinter able to match Bobby Morrow's gold-winning time in 1936 would not make the final in Barcelona in 1992.

Yet while Australians relate easily to this challenge of achieving world-class performance in sport—that is, of being fully internationally competitive—they tend not to embrace that same goal in business and for the economy. There are historical reasons for this, but unless our attitudes change and we face up to the challenge and match it with the world, we will not maintain, let alone improve, Australia's standard of living.

The Business Athlete reminds us that for the nation to develop and achieve a vision of superior economic performance requires individuals to develop a personal dedication to superior individual performances in their work. Work gets done through people, and improvements are made by people. Corporations that want to succeed into the next century have put a good deal of effort over recent years into organisational and cultural change, and these changes have as their central goal the creation of structures, systems and support to enable individuals to maximise their contributions to the business. Getting the structures and systems right will assist but, in the end, performance comes down to the individual, with the most important prerequisite for excellence being the right mindset—a combination of vision, dedication and motivation. I had the pleasure of meeting a number of Australia's Olympic athletes and aspiring young athletes during the time I was president of the Melbourne candidature to host the 1996 Olympic Games. Whatever their sport, they shared a vision of being the best that they could be.

The Business Athlete draws direct parallels between sport and business and builds the profile of a business athlete as similar to top-class sporting athletes. They share mindsets. They can also share much in the fields of motivation, goals, tactics and techniques. They have much in common in terms of approaching and preparing themselves for their own personal-best performances.

As with Olympic athletes, the vision of excellence for business should be a global vision. Why would people in business aim for a level of competition other than the top league? Yet in economic terms Australia is in danger of being relegated, and too many people seem to accept this with complacency or as somehow inevitable. The quest for excellence, as set by the best in the world, should drive the goals of business athletes.

In the chapter entitled, 'A Vision of Excellence' we read

> Athletes in sport and business are reluctant to accept the status quo and are never satisfied with mediocrity.

In our company, CRA, we put it this way

> Achieving continuous improvement starts, essentially, with a state of mind that accepts that there are always better ways of doing things and that there is always room to improve everything we do.

We also say that the real meaning of being internationally competitive is that we must continually improve what we do in order 'to meet changing customer needs better than competitors'. The concept of a constantly improving international competitive field is one we seek to convey to all our employees.

In business, one current expression for 'know the competition' is 'benchmarking'—studying competitors' operations, their systems, their ways of working in order to see how we measure up and areas where improvement can be achieved. Athletes know that not only is performance best measured relative to competition, but that there is much to be learned from studying one's competitors.

Sport psychology is evolving rapidly and spreading fast as an important element in performance enhancement by athletes. This book takes some of the specific, practical tools and techniques now being successfully implemented by athletes and suggests ways they could be applied by business athletes to enhance their own performances.

The key to this is self-knowledge—recognising and understanding what constitutes one's own top performances and what specific amalgam of conditions, when created, will be most conducive to achieving an outstanding personal business performance and result.

I believe the authors are correct in identifying that 'Excellence is the end result of a process'. Focussing on the process is more important than focussing on the outcome. The process will usually incorporate a myriad of little things, which *The Business Athlete* explores, things such as realistic goal-setting with subgoals and timelines, having a game plan and back-up plans, team relationships, appropriate feedback mechanisms, conducting review sessions, practice runs, personal health and techniques for mental calming.

Organisations are working to get structures in place to improve all of these components of the process in order systematically to eliminate events and forces which will detract from the excellence of a company's final outcomes.

Individuals need to take personal responsibility for doing the same. There should be no doubt about the importance of the contribution of each and every individual through improving their work performance, to Australia's economic wellbeing.

The kinds of changes we need to make in Australia are those which capture the incremental improvements. Winners tend not to be determined by big one-off breakthroughs. A step change in competitiveness achieved through technology or research or a major process change can put a company amongst the front runners in a global race. But it is the small constant improvements resulting from the creative efforts of individuals and teams which lifts companies out of the pack and into the medal class and which can keep companies there.

The best athletes, whether in sport or business, work at achieving these small gains, which in the end can make them world beaters. As the authors say in the chapter 'Winning Attitudes'

> Everyday these athletes seek small improvements. They know that as they get closer to the top, the size of these improvements gets less and less. When this happens, they look for even the slightest edge, because that can be the difference between the winner's dais or the loser's locker room.

As with athletes, so with companies and countries. The business game of the future will demand no less.

John Ralph
June 1992

CONTENTS

Acknowledgements		x
Preface		xi
Introduction		xiii
1	Winning attitudes	1
2	Goal selection and action	15
3	A vision of excellence	25
4	Performance quality: A system	31
5	The performance zone	47
6	Active calmness	60
7	A winning focus	73
8	Four performance tools	84
9	Performance imagination	92
10	Breaking down the performance barriers	103
11	Event preparation and review	116
12	Fit body, fit mind	125
13	The business coach	133
14	Summary	141
	Endnotes	143

ACKNOWLEDGEMENTS

Many people have influenced and shaped our lives and in so doing made their own unique contribution to this book. We take this opportunity to thank those people, together with others who have contributed more directly to the book.

To our parents, who sadly cannot be with us but as a result of their love and guidance are very much part of everything we do.

To Carol for her love and support.

To Mark and Ben for being great kids.

To Dr Adrian Porter for being a business athlete in the field of medicine.

To Mr Gene Whitford for leading the way and encouraging us to follow.

To Mr John Ralph for kindly consenting to write the Foreword.

To Mr John Cambridge for his vision and enthusiasm, and Mr Kunio Satake for his thoughtful and perceptive comments.

To our many business and sport clients and colleagues. Their encouragement and endeavours have formed the basis of this book.

PREFACE

The nations of the world have moved. Not geographically, of course, but culturally and economically. Countries like Australia, the United States of America, Britain, Canada and New Zealand have lost what seemed to be their birthright: the right to assume that their standard of living would continue to rise, or at least be maintained.

The countries of the world have moved closer together. The Western world, which saw rapid economic growth in the postwar years, now marches to the beat of a different drum. Information technology, trading blocs, emerging regions and nations, the demise of communism, the global economy—these are different games, played according to different rules on a different playing field.

Contrary to popular opinion, this is not a crossroad: this is a T-junction, and for nations it is time to indicate their intentions. The old road does not lead into the new millennium. Countries will either turn, perform and compete successfully along the new road of international competitiveness, or turn and slow down to greet lower living standards, less internal control over resources and ultimately an uncertain and potentially disastrous future.

There are now no lucky countries, only competitive countries. On the new international playing field, the old players lack the speed, strength and endurance to meet the challenges. A new player is needed: a player who, like the international athlete, is highly skilled, physically and mentally prepared and totally committed to consistent, high quality performance. That new player is the **business athlete**.

Without doubt, the winning nations will be those who fill their schools, their businesses, their governments and their communities with business athletes.

This book creates the concept of the **business athlete** and shows the way onto the new playing fields.

Let the game begin.

INTRODUCTION

The Business Athlete comprises a training process, a way of life and a role model for people working in any field. It is unusual in that it draws its source material and methods from three quite different and yet intricately linked areas.

- In sport, the spirit of enterprise, competition and 'having a go' provides the foundation and offers the challenge to performers in business.

- The applied science of performance in sport provides the models, techniques and tools.

- This mix of spirit and applied science is integrated with the pragmatic reality of day-to-day business life.

The book has been developed from the training program we designed and are currently conducting for business professionals and organisations. Business athlete training is available throughout Australia and New Zealand, as well as many other countries worldwide.

THE PSYCHOLOGY OF PERFORMANCE

In recent years, as world standards in sport have soared, leading professional and Olympic athletes have found that there is more to achieving their ultimate potential than physical fitness and skill. The huge role psychology plays in performance has become evident, to the extent that many athletes and coaches now believe that the only significant difference between world-class athletes is psychological.

As a consequence of demands from coaches and athletes, there has been an astonishing growth in the field of performance psychology. Research has proliferated, scientific journals have been developed and performance psychologists have been called in to work with top athletes in every Olympic and professional sport.

A body of scientific knowledge about the psychology of performance has been formulated and, based on this, psychologists working with athletes and coaches have developed techniques that are now used by leading international competitors.

It is a logical progression to apply this knowledge of performance psychology to other areas and, with the ongoing push for international competitiveness in business, nothing would seem more appropriate than applying the science of performance psychology to creating 'business athletes'.

Business athletes produce consistent, reliable, high quality performance. They work in a team, or as individuals, and are found in all occupations. They are employed in corporations, in small business and in government. They may lead companies, maintain balance sheets, provide professional services or serve behind a counter. Whatever their 'game', business athletes have a vision of being the best that they can be.

FOUR KEY FACTORS
There are four key factors that form the basis for business athlete training and it is important that you are aware of these before beginning the main text of the book.

1. BUSINESS ATHLETE TRAINING IS FOR PERFORMERS
Just as sport psychology training is undertaken on the assumption that an athlete is physically fit, technically skilled and committed to fulfilling their potential, so business athlete training assumes that you are technically or professionally skilled and committed to performance quality.

2. BUSINESS ATHLETE TRAINING IS NOT MOTIVATION TRAINING
Too many self-development programs have been strong on motivation and light on substance. Business athletes take responsibility for their own motivation, and the training builds performance skills on this foundation.

3. THE AIM OF BUSINESS ATHLETE TRAINING IS CONSISTENT, LONG-TERM PROGRESS

Business athletes are interested in performance but not the short-term, 'win at all costs' performance. They want consistent, long-term progress. Many of the performance skills outlined in this book also require consistent practice and application.

4. THERE ARE NO 'SHOULDS' IN BUSINESS ATHLETE TRAINING

Business athlete training is not traditional business-style training. Nowhere in this book are the words 'should' or 'must' used to instruct you. Business athletes take responsibility to choose what is best for them and their organisation.

We trust that you will enjoy this book and find it stimulating, challenging and informative. More than anything else, however, we trust that it will help you to make an increasingly important contribution to your family, community, organisation and country as a business athlete.

1

WINNING ATTITUDES

> Winning business athletes are totally committed to performance quality for themselves, their team and their organisation.

The difference between leading international athletes is so slight that success is more often determined by attitude than by sporting skill or physical fitness. On their best day any number of athletes can win; however, the champions perform consistently at, or close to, their best.

Top athletes continually search for ways to create a more consistent, high quality performance under all types of conditions. This includes competing in different countries and simulating the demands of competition throughout their training program.

Every day these athletes seek small improvements. They know that as they get closer to the top, the size of these improvements diminishes. When this happens they look for even the slightest edge, because that can be the difference between the winner's dais or the loser's locker room.

The champions also use competition to learn more about their sport, their opponents and their own reactions. This helps them to understand how to *trigger* their best performances in big competitions.

Top athletes seek quality results and achieve these through a commitment to quality and self-development at all stages of their training.

Business athletes can learn a lot from these attitudes because they are fundamental to all types of performance. They apply to stage performers such as the great opera singers, to the clerk at the front counter of the local bank, and to the chief executive of a multinational corporation. Each one is an athlete in their own field and each can make a commitment to developing a winning attitude in themselves and their team.

Business performance is usually measured over many years. Name 100 successful people or organisations and you can be sure that most, if not all of them, have been putting a good performance together for a long time. They might have made a breakthrough 'overnight', but if you look beyond their highest achievements there is likely to be a history of consistent, quality effort. Certainly the long-term vision and patient approach of the Japanese in industry vividly illustrates this vital principle.

Consistency, reliability and regular improvement are critical to achieving your long-term progress and success. Just as athletes continue to learn about themselves and their sport, so too do the business athletes continue to learn about their 'playing field' and themselves.

How does your current attitude measure up to the descriptions above?

How do your team members' attitudes measure up?

Have you got a team of consistent, high quality performers?

THE NEW PLAYER
There is always a young, up-and-coming player.

In sport, the new player is often brash, aggressive, confident and eager to 'knock off' one of the top players.

In business, new players look for ways to secure a foothold in the market, sometimes taking an existing market share through price-cutting or finding a niche where they can be competitive. For example, when the Japanese first entered the American market they used the strategy of selling lower-priced imitations of local goods. From that point they added improvements to products and service and, through continual innovation and improvement, moved steadily over two decades from the bottom end of the market to market domination in many key industries such as computers, electrical goods and motor vehicles.

Good new players often motivate the existing players to redouble their efforts, to experiment with new ideas and approaches, or to capitalise fully on their own strengths. Top players aren't threatened by new players but instead use the opportunity to fine-tune their own performance.

Interestingly, in the computing industry most innovations over the past decade came from relatively new organisations. These included Apple Computers with the micro, Digital with the mini and Conner Peripherals with the 2.5 inch drive for 'notebook' computers.

In women's tennis, Martina Navratilova introduced a more aggressive serve-and-volley game to break the hold which Chris Evert had on the world's number one position, and we all remember how *Australia II* capitalised on the real and psychological advantage gained from the winged keel to win the America's Cup.

One of the keys to the success of new players in sport and business is that they don't accept existing limitations: they want to get to the top and they focus all of their efforts on making a breakthrough.

It is important for businesses that have existed for some time to create an environment within their own organisation which fosters the development of new players. In the business athlete training conducted in industry, participating organisations undertake simulated and real-life activities that assist them to understand and implement this principle.

What are the existing limitations in your field?

Is someone going to ignore those limitations and 'go for it' anyway?

KEY ATTITUDES OF LEADING ATHLETES
The remainder of this chapter explores just a few of the key attitudes displayed by leading athletes in sport and business.

MOTIVATION TO ACHIEVE
Successful athletes typically have a strong desire to achieve. They seek and enjoy tangible measured success, such as winning a football premiership or an Olympic gold medal.

In business, the rewards can also be tangible; for example, sales results, revenue increases, cost savings, satisfied customers. Many companies use these as scoreboards or targets to motivate their business athletes. This can be highly effective, although it is important to emphasise that this is not for everyone. One of the premises behind the training of top athletes in sport and business is that each is an individual and there are many different ways to achieve the same aim of high quality, consistent performance.

The adrenalin rush

Achievement-driven athletes tend to experience lower anxiety levels than their less-achievement-driven colleagues. They particularly enjoy facing challenging, competitive situations where there is a balanced chance of winning or losing. For professional athletes such as basketballers, this means enjoying the adrenalin rush of playing against high quality opposition in front of big crowds in important games. Many top athletes thrive on this type of situation.

Perhaps the business equivalents of professional basketballers are the property developers, the international commodity dealers and the creative directors of major advertising firms who put themselves in win/lose situations every day.

Can you think of other business situations where the players thrive on challenge, competition and the adrenalin rush?

Performance monitoring

Achievement-driven athletes want to know how they are performing and they keep their coaches very busy providing them with performance statistics such as times, number of possessions, comparisons with others, tactical successes and so on. These athletes wear heart rate monitors during training and arrange to have training and competition videotaped. They monitor every aspect of performance in the search for another edge.

Business has typically looked at bottom-line or end-result statistics to provide performance information. Doctors look at the end result of an operation, shopkeepers study monthly profit and loss statements, and sales managers look at new business for each major period.

Many of the performance statistics used in business are like the overall time for a distance runner. They are gross figures that do not discriminate between the various small processes which make up a performance. Athletes have recognised this and they now measure heart rate, stride length, muscle tension, pre-performance moods and times for each segment. Similarly, business athletes are not content to just accept the information they receive but rather they look for better sources of more immediate information which help them to understand the components of their performance.

Think about an important objective that you need to achieve as a part of your work responsibilities. There are many small steps or tasks you will complete to achieve that objective. The greater the precision with which you are able to measure your performance on each of these processes, the better will be your prospects of a positive result.

Other sources of motivation

While the desire to achieve is strong amongst athletes in sport and business, there are, of course, many other sources of motivation.

How many of the following are important to you?

- the task or activity itself, for example, hitting a ball or programming a computer
- the satisfaction of doing something competently
- meeting and working with other people
- self-improvement/development
- recognition from other people

To foster your own motivation in sport or business use the following affirmations as a checklist.

- I have realistic and challenging goals.
- I have a strategy for achieving each of my major goals.
- I visualise my goals being achieved.
- I regularly feed my mind with positive information; for example, read books, watch videotapes, talk with positive people, regularly review and reset my goals.
- I enjoy my successes.
- I maintain balance in my life.

What do you currently do to develop and sustain your achievement motivation?

A WILLINGNESS TO MAKE SACRIFICES

To be the best at anything requires considerable investment of resources such as time, money and effort. This applies to an individual athlete, a team, a major business corporation and a business athlete.

An athlete who makes a decision to allocate a resource to achieving a sporting goal is also making a decision to sacrifice something else. A highly motivated athlete may not see these as sacrifices but nevertheless the following example shows how this is the case.

Swimmers who set their sights on making the Olympic swim team might allocate 25 hours per week to training and another 5 hours for travelling to and from training. Some of the sacrifices made by the swimmers include all of the potential activities which they may have been involved in during those 30 hours. These could include other sport and recreation activities, studies, career opportunities, favourite foods, social life, time spent in one's own country and sleep.

The level of performance an athlete reaches is strongly influenced by the type and number of sacrifices that he or she is prepared to make.

In business, a significant achievement in one area will also almost inevitably have a cost in another. Some areas which you might consider before committing to career goals include:

- family
- social activities
- travel
- sporting career
- hobbies

> Business athletes recognise that there are always things to be given up or sacrificed in return for success. Sometimes these sacrifices are worthwhile and sometimes they are not. Business athletes make this judgement in consultation with their families and other people whose opinion they value.

What sacrifices are you prepared to make to achieve your most important goals?

COMMITMENT
Commitment is one of the buzz words in sport. Few people outside the network of international sport recognise the level

of commitment and consistent effort of athletes training and competing at that level. To provide an insight into the extent of this commitment, the following is an example of a training week which might be completed by a cyclist preparing to compete at Olympic level.

CYCLING TRAINING PROGRAM

DAY	TIME	TRAINING LOAD
Sunday	7.30 am	180 km: 40 km hill climbing 20 km fast on undulations 120 km steady pace
Monday	6.30 am 8.30 am 4.00 pm	25 min on rollers 160 km on road (steady pace) weight training
Tuesday	6.30 am 8.00 am	25 min on rollers 240 km on road: 40 km hill climbing 30 km fast on undulations 170 km steady pace
Wednesday	6.30 am 8.00 am 2.30 pm	20 min on rollers 125 km on road (steady pace) weight training
Thursday	6.30 am 8.00 am 4.00 pm	30 min on rollers 150 km on road (steady pace) 4 X 15 min on exercise bike (fast intervals)
Friday	8.00 am 12.00 noon	120 km on road (steady pace) weight training
Saturday	Choice Evening	80 km on road (steady pace) racing

> The secret of success for top athletes is a commitment
> to train harder and prepare better. They refuse to rest
> on the laurels of natural talent.

Interestingly, many top athletes don't like to let others know
just how much extra work they put in, preferring to let them
think that it all comes easily and naturally. When conducting
segments of our 12-month in-house business athlete training
program with corporate clients, we have observed a similar
strategy being used by many business athletes.

Business athletes recognise that to be the best they can
be requires

- a commitment to a goal
- the self-discipline to do what is necessary to achieve that
  goal

Examples of commitment
Commitment can mean many things including

- studying in the evening
- working two jobs
- saying no to a career opportunity which affects family goals
- taking on tasks which aren't glamorous or recognised
- letting someone else take the credit for your work
- tolerating physical discomfort
- being prepared to seek out and accept criticism
- maintaining high quality under difficult conditions

Committed athletes think nothing of devoting hours to
practising one small aspect of their game. A coach of a
professional team with whom we have consulted often tells
his players that professionals keep on practising a skill until
they get it right every time. This type of commitment to
total quality is the foundation on which many successful
coaches and athletes have built their careers.

Here are some other examples of business athletes showing
commitment.

- A human resources manager visits a staff member in hospital.
- A carpenter takes extra time to get the finished product
  just right.
- A taxi driver works from 5.30 am to 6.30 pm six days per
  week to put his children through college.

- An accountant pores over new government legislation for hours to fully understand and apply it appropriately for clients.
- A check-out operator at a supermarket offers to replace a damaged item which hadn't been noticed by the customer.
- A country medical practitioner is on call seven days a week.

What does commitment mean to you?
To what are you committed?

Business athletes do all that is asked of them and then put in that little bit extra, to make sure that they get the winning edge.

PERSEVERANCE

Very few athletes reach the top in their sport without years of perseverance. An excellent example of perseverance and consistent, high quality effort is golfer Jack Nicklaus, whose major championship victories spanned 27 years.

In business and in sport, perseverance means:

- keeping the main goal in sight
- maintaining quality effort over a long period of time
- continually learning from even the greatest disappointments
- bouncing back from setbacks
- encouraging yourself and others to keep going
- not letting discouragement affect effort level

The ability to persevere under duress, and to maintain standards even when the ultimate goal is out of sight, is something which separates the champions from the 'shooting stars'. An example of this, again from golf, is the performance of Curtis Strange in the 1988 British Open. Strange shot an 80 in the first round, but rather than giving up after this poor performance followed it with rounds of 69, 69 and 68 to finish in a creditable 13th place.

The business athlete recognises that most things of significance are achieved with persistence over a lengthy period of time.

EAGER TO LEARN

Olympic athletes, particularly those who compete in endurance sports, such as the triathlon, distance running and rowing, are often fanatical in their search for knowledge about themselves and training methods.

Self-knowledge

Heart rate monitors are used by athletes to measure their training load. They use the information on heart rates to better understand their own body's reaction to training, and to train at an optimal level. Physiological and psychological tests are also employed in top sport. Athletes regularly complete tests which provide vital information on their current performance.

Sport knowledge

Top athletes keep up to date with developments in sport science. They learn to select the information relevant to them and apply it to improve their performance. To fulfil potential and be competitive at the top level requires that athletes continually add to their knowledge about themselves and their sport.

Top athletes also look for opportunities to compete against others, or to better their own standards. Training will prepare them up to a point, but they need to compete in order to fine-tune their skills.

Business athlete knowledge

You can take a lead from our top athletes by

- measuring your performance
- keeping up to date with developments in your profession
- using relevant information to increase the performance of yourself and your team

Business athletes are committed to ongoing education and self-development. Like the Olympic athlete, they filter out the information which is relevant to them and put this to practical use. They look for feedback about their performance and then use this to improve their performance in the future.

Successful business athletes utilise many sources of feedback including

- statistics—for example, sales, performance against budget
- a performance appraisal interview
- peer review
- discussions with clients/customers
- discussions with superiors
- staff comments
- self-review
- a health assessment conducted by a doctor or physiologist

Which of these sources of feedback can you utilise?

Education

Education for the business athlete can include

- formal study, for example for a business degree such as an MBA
- selected seminars or courses, for example, 'Train the Trainer'
- on-the-job experience

Business athletes do not complete their education and self-development when they finish at school or university. This doesn't necessarily mean further formal study, but it does mean that they act as any professional does, by continually updating their knowledge and skills.

What commitment do you currently make to furthering your skills and knowledge?

RISK-TAKING

Physical risks

Many top athletes are attracted to their sport by the inherent dangers, for example ski jumping and motorbike racing, or by the physical contact such as in rugby and boxing. These athletes enjoy activities where there is risk of physical injury. They react to these situations by 'going for it' in a very positive way.

Psychological risks

Athletes are also attracted to situations of psychological risk, which means performing in public and pitting their skills directly against others. Here the risk can include embarrassment, loss of privacy, personal abuse and so on.

Business risks

In business, the risks are not usually physical, although the effects of long-term stress and pressure have been linked to physical illness. The risks to the business athlete can fall into various categories; however, the two principal categories identified by participants completing business athlete training are psychological and financial.

Financial risks were played down to a large extent in the 1980s. Credit was easy to obtain, and many entrepreneurs happily risked and lost other people's money. The business athlete is an ethical person who recognises and accepts responsibility for risks taken. These risks are well conceived and, as with an athlete, are only made after a thorough preparation.

The **psychological risks** you face as a business athlete are largely determined by you. For example, a friend may view a change of employment as a major risk, while you could see it as a logical move. Situations which for some people might lead to embarrassment, loss of face, or fear of failure, can be challenging and stimulating to others. Put simply, the extent of the risk is determined by your attitude.

Experience reduces the risk

In sport, the football halfback watches the play and makes judgments about when and where to move. He has learnt how to do this from experience. The business athlete watches the business game and through experience learns when and how to make a move.

> The business athlete is pro-active and takes calculated risks.

PREPARED FOR 'NO PAIN NO GAIN'

Most football club weight training rooms have a sign somewhere which says, 'No pain, no gain'. In the lead up to the Barcelona Olympics in 1992, many athletes also added the thoughtful theme, 'No pain, no Spain'. Suffice to say that physical fitness, to the level required for top level sport, is not achieved without pain.

Even the laziest of athletes will grudgingly admit that the greatest benefits of physical training usually come when their muscles are hurting and their lungs feel that they are about to explode.

It is not necessary to feel like that at work but the adage still holds true in that few worthwhile achievements occur without some setbacks. Some pathways are going to be more difficult, however, these may have the greatest rewards at the end. Keep your goal in mind and, like the athlete, take pride in your ability to push through the tough patches.

AN EXPECTATION OF SUCCESS
When our leading athletes compete, they expect to do well. It is this positive attitude that further increases the likelihood that they will achieve the success that they desire. The positive attitude and the associated self-confidence is the consequence of years of training and competitive success.

There are also other keys to developing this attitude of expecting success. Try some of these:

- think and believe that you are important
- dress like a successful person
- talk about success
- turn defeats into success
- refuse to let irrational fear get in the way of achieving important goals

Business athletes expect to do well and they visualise themselves being successful. Their attitude is then the precursor to the success which follows. They set and achieve goals and this reinforces their feelings of competence.

Do you expect to succeed?

DOMINANCE
When an athlete like decathlon champion Daley Thompson walks onto the track, spectators are left in no doubt that they are looking at a champion. Every movement portrays confidence and dominance.

Most top performers let their opponents know who is boss through their body language and overall style.

Do you act like the Daley Thompson of your workplace or profession?

Business athletes portray an image appropriate to their goals and position. This includes dressing, speaking and acting in a way which is consistent with the image that they wish to project.

A common theme amongst business athletes is that they appear to be dominant in their profession. This doesn't mean that they necessarily dominate other people, but rather that they project an aura of self assurance and self-worth.

BUSINESS ATHLETE AFFIRMATIONS

Athletes use positive self-statements or affirmations to create the performance attitudes they desire. Each chapter of *The Business Athlete* finishes with statements used in business athlete training programs in industry, and we have included them to help you to begin integrating the concepts from that particular chapter into your daily rituals. The following statements are based on the concepts in this chapter. Use them regularly.

- 'My long-term progress and success are based on consistency, reliability and regular improvement.'
- 'I am continually learning and developing.'
- 'I don't just accept existing limitations.'
- 'I monitor each aspect of my performance in the search for another edge.'
- 'I produce my best by committing to important goals and having the discipline to achieve them.'
- 'I am totally committed to quality in myself, my team and my organisation.'
- 'I expect to do well and visualise myself being successful'
- 'I look, act and am successful.'

2

GOAL SELECTION AND ACTION

Goals give business athletes a 'scoreboard' against
which to assess performance: they encourage
motivation, energy and persistence.

WHY GOAL-SETTING?

Goal-setting is the most widely used and researched performance enhancement technique. Hundreds of studies have explored the effects of goals on performance, and results show that goal-setting is a valid and extremely effective way of improving performance.[1] Having said this, however, it is also important to add that ineffective goal-setting can and does lead to reduced performance.

There are four good reasons why goals enhance performance and therefore why leading athletes and business athletes set goals.

1. GOALS PROVIDE DIRECTION

Goals provide a sense of direction and purpose. When an athlete says, 'My most important goal is to get selected in the national team to compete at the world championships next year', this helps to focus their effort. Similarly, when a business athlete says, 'My most important goal is to find one major new account by the end of June', this gives clear direction and therefore the necessary resources such as time, marketing materials and people can be allocated in the most effective way.

Do your goals currently provide you with a sense of direction and purpose?

2. GOALS ARE MOTIVATING

Goal-setting is the most recognised motivational tool available in sport and business. Athletes who aim to compete in the Olympics use the vision of achieving this goal to motivate themselves to train harder. Goals are a major source of motivation in sport and business.

Do you currently have a goal that motivates you?

3. GOALS ENCOURAGE PERSISTENCE

The members of the Olympic-medal-winning Australian cycling team train for up to eight hours per day, including hill climbing, track riding, weight circuits and psychology training. In 12 months they cover 38,000 kilometres on the road, much of it in the mountains of Italy, Mexico and the United States of America. This requires enormous persistence. Unquestionably their goals—to be competitive in Olympic Games and world championships—encourage this persistence.

Do your goals provide encouragement to persist through the tough times?

4. GOALS LEAD TO STRATEGIES

A goal such as 'to win an Olympic medal' encourages athletes to devise a set of strategies for achieving that goal. These strategies might include training plans, competition schedules, rearrangement of other activities, and so on. The strategies might even seem a bit extreme, like Bruce Jenner, the American Olympic decathlon champion, who had a hurdle in his lounge room so that he could train at home.

Do you have clear strategic plans for achieving your high priority goals?

> Learning and using the skill of goal-setting is the most important first step in becoming a business athlete.

KEYS TO SETTING EFFECTIVE GOALS

The notion of goal-setting is not new. In our experience, however, most people when offered the suggestion, 'Set a goal', find this advice to be rather trite. Unfortunately, most athletes and business people *don't* make full use of goal-setting, despite believing that they do. Typically, they fail to follow the basic principles of using goals for performance enhancement.

These basic principles are:

1. ASSESS YOUR PRESENT LEVEL

Olympic, professional and business athletes have a clearly planned set of goals that show them where they are going today, tomorrow, next week, next month, next year and maybe even next decade. These goals are based on a knowledge of possible goals and a systematic analysis of personal (and team) strengths and limitations.

Have you assessed your major strengths and limitations in light of your goals?

2. MAKE YOUR GOALS SPECIFIC

The major reason athletes and business athletes fail to use goal-setting effectively is that they set goals that are too general. For example, tennis players who say, 'I want to improve my concentration during matches', are unlikely to improve their concentration as much as if they phrased the goal more specifically, such as, 'I want to be able to play three full sets, without losing my focus on playing one point at a time'.

In business, instead of phrasing a goal as, 'I plan to improve my time management', it could be made more effective by rephrasing as, 'I plan to use a diary system and rearrange my office filing system by the end of next week'.

Business athletes set specific goals because they provide something definite to work towards. This makes it easier to be organised and to measure progress.

Are your current goals specific?

> The best goals are specific.

3. MAKE YOUR GOALS CHALLENGING

Most athletes and coaches know that challenging goals produce the best results. A goal that is too easy does not create enough enthusiasm, drive and energy, but if a goal is too difficult to achieve, athletes lose interest and self-confidence.

In business it is customary to set budgets at a high level, although many companies now set sales quotas at levels that a high percentage of their sales staff can achieve. This makes sense, because it ensures that more people will succeed, and success then breeds further success.

This contrasts with a well-known consulting firm who, after a very successful year, decided to increase all quotas by 30 per cent, despite a looming recession. This was one of the reasons that over 75 per cent of the professional staff left within the 12 months.

Are your important goals realistic and challenging?

Business athletes select goals that are challenging and able to be achieved with some effort.

---

4. MAKE YOUR GOALS FLEXIBLE

Athletes learn early in their careers that no one can be guaranteed success every time they compete. In some sports, success can be very elusive, even for the top players. For example, on the professional golf circuit there was a period of nearly four years in which no player won more than one major title.

Success can also come at the most unexpected times, as John Daly, winner of the 1991 USA PGA championship, found. Daly gained a late, unexpected entry into the event, because Nick Price withdrew to be with his wife for the birth of their child. Subsequently, Daly led the field for the final three rounds, leaving everyone else in his wake.

The unpredictability of sport requires athletes and teams to be able to adjust goals according to their successes and failures. For example, if a basketballer sets a goal to average 20 points per game for the next month, what does he do if he shoots 40 points in each of the first two games? Even if he doesn't score in the remaining two games he will still have his average. Top athletes faced with this situation reset their goals for the remaining two games to average more than 20 points for these games.

A business athlete, working in life assurance sales, may have committed to a goal of writing $30,000 of premium income over a 2-month period. If she has a very successful first week and writes half this total, then she will adjust her goals so that they are still challenging and therefore motivating.

If your team sets a goal to complete a project by the end of the month and then, through objective measurement, recognises that the project will take much longer, it is sensible performance management to reschedule the goal or allocate additional resources.

Business athletes recognise that working towards personal or team goals which have become too difficult can create unnecessary pressure that affects quality. Similarly, goals that are too easy to achieve can lead to complacency.

Are you prepared to adjust your goals when circumstances change?

5. SELECT A NUMBER OF GOALS

One of the reasons that top athletes like golfer Jack Nicklaus and sprinter Carl Lewis are self-confident is because they have had a lot of success during their careers. Success builds confidence, which in turn leads to even greater success.

Athletes recognise the boost in confidence which can come from success and regularly break their major goals into sub-goals, thereby increasing the number of goals that they achieve. This means more success, and consequently more self-confidence.

One of the keys to business athletes' self-confidence is the boost they gain from regularly setting and achieving daily, weekly and long-term goals. Business athletes managing a department might set goals such as those that are listed here.

- achieve annual budget
- achieve monthly budget targets
- reduce stock levels by 10 per cent
- improve personal organisation by 20 per cent
- rearrange display cabinets to highlight new products
- communicate better with staff—hold weekly meetings
- manage stress levels by practising calming techniques

What goals are you working towards this next week?

6. PUT YOUR GOALS IN WRITING

Olympic athletes use specially designed performance diaries to record their competition and training goals, strategies and experiences. These diaries encourage athletes to divide major goals such as 'win the national championship' into daily goals such as 'complete 120 kilometres on road today' for training and competition.

> Immediate (daily) or short-term (weekly) goals are generally more effective in enhancing performance.

Business athletes use their diaries as performance management tools. In their diaries they record a range of information including

- appointments
- things to do
- expenses
- ideas, plans and strategies
- reviews of performance
- reminders

How can you make greater use of your diary as a goal-setting and performance management tool?

7. USE POSITIVE GOALS

Most golfers will tell you that it is better to be positive and say, 'My goal is to hit the fairway', rather than to choose the negative, such as, 'My goal is to stay out of the trees'. When you set a positive goal it transmits an image of the positive outcome to your brain, thereby increasing the chances of that result occurring. On the other hand, when you say what you don't want to happen, it sends an image of the negative, for example, hitting the ball into the trees.

Some examples of negative goals commonly seen in business include:

'We can't afford to lose another client.'
'The boss says to finish this, or else!'
'I musn't make a mistake.'
'I hope our competitors don't win that deal.'

Goal-setting works best when positive goals are selected. The exception to this is when doing something in which you are already very skilled. For example, if you are very familiar with adding up your weekly expense sheet but tend to make careless mistakes, then set a goal to make no errors.

Needless to say, if you are making an important presentation to the board, it is far better to focus on a positive goal than to tell yourself not to make an error.

Are your goals positive?

DESIGNING AN INDIVIDUAL GOAL PROGRAM

The following individual goal program is modelled on the program used by professional and Olympic athletes. In the business athlete training programs run in industry, a detailed goal-setting approach is presented in a workbook which is then completed by participants.

A goal-setting program is most effective when it includes goals for all life areas. The reason for this is that high quality performance will only be sustained over extended periods of time when there is a balance between the key aspects of your life.

There are five steps in constructing your individual goal program.

1. Develop an inventory of goals.
2. Choose priorities and time frames.
3. Break the big goals into small goals.
4. Create some action.
5. Keep a check on progress.

It is recommended that you follow the steps and write your responses to the questions and other activities in a diary for later reference.

1. DEVELOP AN INVENTORY OF GOALS

The first step in goal-setting is to develop an *inventory of possible goals*. Refer to each of the eight headings which follow and note down any goals you want to achieve in those areas. The aim is to develop a very broad list of possible goals. Keep the list with you over the next few days and add to it as other goals come to mind.

2. CHOOSE PRIORITIES AND TIME FRAMES

Now that you have developed an inventory of goals, go back over the list, note the time frame and prioritise each goal using the rating list below:

A = high priority   D = not very important
B = important   E = not at all important
C = somewhat important

For example:

GOAL	TIME FRAME	PRIORITY
To run a marathon in under 3 hours	2 years	B
Complete bridge construction plan	3 months	A

3. BREAK THE BIG GOALS INTO SMALL GOALS

Convert each major long-term goal into short-term goals. The short-term goals will provide a more immediate focus for your efforts and will help you to maintain motivation through some of those times when progress is slower.

The examples and activities in the next section link the choice of sub-goals with the setting of action plans.

4. CREATE SOME ACTION

Top athletes convert their goals into action. They know that goals only have real value when action is being taken to achieve them. Go through your inventory of goals and select those which have been given the highest priority. Take each one in turn, and develop at least three action plans for each.

Two examples follow.

GOAL	PRIORITY	TIME FRAME	ACTION PLAN
Double my income.	B	Within 2 years	1 Complete business athlete training. 2 Increase call rate by 20 per cent. 3 Qualify prospects more thoroughly.

GOAL	PRIORITY	TIME FRAME	ACTION PLAN
Spend more quality time with my family.	A	Now	1 Plan my leisure time. 2 Go away with family on weekends once every two months. 3 Leave the office at 5.00 pm on at least one day per week.

5. KEEP A CHECK ON PROGRESS

Business athletes are goal directed. They are sure of their goals and never lose sight of them. They regularly monitor progress and reset their goals as necessary.

Write your major long-term goals in a prominent position in your diary. For example, many business athletes record their short-term goals in the weekly or monthly sections where they can easily check their progress.

WEEKLY AND DAILY GOAL-SETTING

To integrate the technique of goal-setting into your regular routines, take a few minutes at a specific time each week to write down your goals for the coming week.

When you have done this, break these goals down into a plan for the first day of the week.

On each evening allocate a few minutes to doing your plan for the next day.

Review your progress each week.

This approach will help you to make good use of your limited time and energy. This is vital in establishing a foundation for the important performance skills which follow.

TEAM GOALS

The main focus of this chapter has been on developing an individual goal program to create a structure to support the concepts and techniques which follow.

It is important to stress, however, that the principles of effective goal-setting and the processes you have completed can also be applied to business teams. In fact, team goal-setting is essential to overall business performance.

In business athlete training conducted in industry, considerable emphasis is placed on ensuring that team goals and individual goals are compatible. This is most important because businesses cannot afford to have individual performers doing their own thing to the detriment of the total performance.

BUSINESS ATHLETE AFFIRMATIONS

The following affirmations will help you to begin integrating the concepts from this chapter into your daily rituals. Use them regularly.

- 'I use goal-setting as the foundation of my performance management system.'
- 'My confidence is building every day as I set and achieve my goals.'
- 'My goals are specific, challenging, positive and important.'
- 'I maintain consistent, high quality performance by ensuring that there is a balance between the key aspects of my life.'
- 'I integrate goal-setting into my daily rituals.'

3

A VISION OF EXCELLENCE

> Business athletes develop a vision which provides the
> power and energy to construct their future in the way
> that they choose.

THE LINK BETWEEN SPORT AND BUSINESS

On Sunday, 5 April 1896 Baron Pierre De Coubertin saw
his vision of the modern Olympic Games realised.
Remarkably, the existence of the Games today is largely the
result of this man's vision to recreate the Olympics in the
tradition of the ancient Greek Games.

De Coubertin saw the Games as a vehicle and a symbol
of the educational and personal development that can result
from participation in sport. For him, sport was a means of
preparing athletes for their later careers and this ideal is still
seen today in the rules of amateurism, which imply that
Olympic athletes have a profession outside their sport.

The concept of the business athlete borrows from the vision
of people like De Coubertin who have seen sport as a model
and training ground for life. While business athletes perform
on different 'playing fields', the similarities in approach are
striking.

Athletes in sport and business are reluctant to accept the
status quo and are never satisfied with mediocrity. Each, in
their own way, is a performer, competing against someone
or something and eager to fulfil their goals and perhaps their
dreams.

THE POWER OF A VISION

For many athletes their sporting dreams remain exactly that:
dreams. For some, however, the dream becomes a vision to

which they commit their lives for many years to come. That vision might be to compete at the Olympics, to represent State or country, or to make it on a professional circuit.

A business vision might be to lead a company, invent a product, specialise in a field of science, provide better service, be the best in that field, and so on.

In sport and business it is the vision which, like the engine of a Formula One racing car, provides the drive and power.

THE QUEST FOR EXCELLENCE

The foundation of each athlete's vision is the quest for excellence. This is always individual excellence and, where appropriate, team excellence.

Athletes define excellence in two ways:

1. better than others
2. the best that I (we) can be

The power of such a vision to mobilise people and other resources cannot be overestimated. Do you remember the America's Cup defence and challenge in Fremantle, Western Australia, in 1987? The 17 competing syndicates were estimated to have spent a total of $210 million in an attempt to win the Cup. Certainly this is sport and business mixed inexorably together.

Perhaps a more striking example of the power of a vision on an individual is that of Lis Hartel, formerly one of Denmark's pre-eminent equestrians. In 1944, Lis, 23 years old and pregnant, was diagnosed as having polio. Just before the paralysis claimed control of her body and destroyed many of her muscles, Lis gave birth to a daughter.

Lis worked with physiotherapists and doctors, learning to use other muscles. Slowly, through countless hours of courageous and disciplined effort, she recovered sufficiently to ride a horse. Remarkably, in 1952, Lis competed in the Helsinki Games and won a silver medal. To receive her medal she had to be assisted onto the dais by the winner of the gold medal.

Business athletes aim to develop a vision or mission which can be visualised and stated very clearly. The late Robert Holmes à Court provided a good example of a clear and simple vision statement when he said:

My goal is business. It's not politics; it is not scientific-research philosophy; it is not a lot of things. It is one thing: business.[2]

Organisations typically have a vision or mission and business athletes are attracted towards organisations that have a vision compatible with their own.

Similarly, in sport, athletes are attracted towards those sports in which they can achieve their goals or vision. For some athletes, like Victorian and Australian cricketer Simon O'Donnell, this can mean deciding between two very attractive options—international cricket or life as a national football star.

Countries also have a vision, although Australia has generally failed to consolidate and project this over the past two decades. By contrast, the small island country Singapore, one of the economic success stories of the world, has used sporting images and language to express a part of its vision.

We compete in the race of nations, whether we like it or not. We have done quite well competing in the second league. The next step is to make it to the top league. Our competitors are already doing that. Unless we do the same we will be left behind.[3]

This quotation comes from a most impressive publication, which uses as its title a sporting analogy: *The Next Lap*. How appropriate for a country seeking to develop business athletes.

WHAT IS THE ESSENCE OF A VISION?

A vision is not created overnight. It comes just as much from an indefinable, internal desire or drive as from any external reward or influence. It is difficult to capture the essence of a vision in words; however, the following quotation from world-acclaimed athletics coach Percy Cerutty contains many of the elements present in a powerful vision.

It [intensity] is evidenced by great natural powers of endurance or power to survive: the body, in the beginning, may be weakly, but the spirit will be strong. The will to survive will be strong: the intellect will be powerful and instinctively know much that makes for survival. There will be an intense enthusiasm for life—a zest for living, a dissatisfaction with the status quo, a wonderment, interest and identification with all things human and natural. The appetite for know-how will be unquenchable.[4]

There are at least six components that we have found to exist consistently in the visions of top performers in sport and business. These are explained using the key words or elements contained in the previous quotation.

Spirit: A vision does not have to start from a strong position. You may, in fact, choose to achieve in an area which is currently a weakness. As Cerutty highlights, it is not the capacity at the start that is the key but rather the spirit to endure whatever is necessary to realise the vision.

Enthusiasm: The power of a vision is in the energy and enthusiasm which it creates. The greater the moral or personal cause, the greater the desire your vision will create. An excellent example can be seen in the words of the President of the United States, George Bush, at the time of the Gulf War in 1991, when he emphasised over and over the importance of a 'new world order'. By framing the war as a 'moral cause', Bush was attempting to excite and motivate the troops throughout what may have been a protracted campaign. The drive and enthusiasm of Olympic athletes also highlights that the power of a vision is most surely the enthusiasm it can generate and sustain.

Dissatisfaction: The desire to get on with things and to do better is represented in the Olympic motto, '*Citius, altius, fortius*' or Faster, higher, stronger. One of the most graphic examples of this came in the high jump at the Mexico City Olympics in 1968. Dick Fosbury won the gold medal with a completely radical technique which later became known as the Fosbury Flop. So effective was the technique that by 1980 13 out of the 16 Olympic finalists used the Fosbury Flop. Similarly, in business, many great careers have been born out of dissatisfaction with the status quo.

Appetite: Cerutty identified the unquenchable appetite for know-how. When reading Cerutty's book, we were left with the clear opinion that Cerutty did not mean knowledge when he said 'know-how', but rather the *application* of knowledge. For athletes in sport and business, the desire to fulfil their potential includes increasing knowledge about themselves, and applying this to achieving even higher levels of performance.

Patience: For an Olympic athlete, the fact that the Games are held only once every four years makes patience a necessity. Business is most certainly an endurance event in which a vision can span a lifetime. Undoubtedly there are few visions of any consequence in sport or business that are achieved without setbacks or obstacles. Patience is an essential quality.

Courage: The final component of vision is courage. Courage is situation-specific. For example, climbing a mountain can be courageous, so can making a sales call on a tough prospect or staying calm when a customer is abusive.

> Top athletes in sport and business have the courage to do what is necessary to achieve their vision.

So there they are. Six key words, used by the business athlete and available to you to assess, to develop and to measure your vision:

- spirit
- enthusiasm
- dissatisfaction
- appetite
- patience
- courage

As a final comment, consider the words of Olympic and world decathlon champion, Daley Thompson:

> I've always thought that everybody can be good at something and it's just a matter of finding it. Most people don't find the thing that they're good at until it's too late. I happened to find it when I was sixteen.[5]

DEVELOPING A BUSINESS ATHLETE VISION
Business athletes develop their vision by:

- associating with top performers
- visualising their desired future
- reading biographies of successful people
- feeding their mind with positive ideas
- avoiding saying 'I can't'
- seeking the help of a mentor
- believing in themselves
- always believing that things can be done better

BUSINESS ATHLETE AFFIRMATIONS
The following positive self-statements will help you to begin integrating the concepts from this chapter into your daily rituals. Use them regularly.

- 'I am reluctant to accept the status quo and will never be satisfied with mediocrity.'
- 'I cultivate a vision of what I want to be.'
- 'The foundation of my vision is the quest for excellence.'
- 'The power of my vision is in the enthusiasm which it generates and sustains.'
- 'My vision is constructed with spirit, enthusiasm, patience, courage, a dissatisfaction with existing ways and an appetite to apply the knowledge which I gain.'

4

PERFORMANCE QUALITY:
A SYSTEM

> High quality performance is the result of high quality
> actions at each stage of the performance process.

Olympic and professional athletes learn early in their careers
that success is not achieved overnight. Rather, it is the result
of many actions or processes which occur over an extended
period of time. The long road to success is clearly illustrated
by the example of Ben Hogan, who is widely recognised as
one of the greatest golfers of all time. Hogan turned professional at the age of 16, endured many setbacks and, through
perseverance, finally won his first major tournament many
years later. Hogan then went on to become a golfing legend.

EXCELLENCE IS A PROCESS, NOT AN OUTCOME
Excellence is the end result of an excellent process. The
various steps that make up the process vary from one sport
to another, just as they vary from one profession to another.
In swimming, for example, the process can include many
of the following:

- a well-planned and well-executed training program
- self-discipline
- an effective pre-event taper
- consistent mental preparation
- a balanced, nutritious diet
- a good start to the race
- rhythm
- a race plan

31

A good business performance is also more often than not the result of a process which includes actions taken over the previous weeks, months or years. For example, business athletes working in a promotional area might identify a process which includes high quality in the following areas:

- market and product research
- developing promotional materials
- identification and qualification of prospects
- contacts with potential clients
- a diary system
- team coordination

Each of these steps can be divided once again into smaller steps. Just as swimmers can look to many small aspects of technique such as stroke, kick and turn, so business athletes can divide an area—for example contacts with potential clients—into smaller aspects such as numbers of contacts, effective listening, identifying needs, matching products to needs, ascertaining capacity to pay and so on.

The important point, which is stressed time and again throughout this book, is that quality performance comes from high quality actions at each stage of the process. In many cases these actions are not easily seen or observed by other people. Business athletes know that these actions are vital to overall performance.

Top athletes in sport and business attend to the little things that form the foundation on which the big achievements are built.

When you look back over some of your better performances, what were the 'little things' upon which that performance was built?

Make a note of these; use them again and again to trigger high quality performance. Above all, remember that business athletes do not take these things for granted.

GET SET TO SUCCEED
Top athletes and teams set themselves up to succeed. They achieve success by arranging themselves and their

surroundings in a way which gives them the best possible opportunity to make the most of their abilities.

This can be seen in the approach of experienced athletes when they arrive in another country. They immediately set out to make themselves feel comfortable and 'at home' by decorating their room with pictures and other personal effects. They then familiarise themselves with the city or town by finding out about transport, shops and banks. The next stage is to become familiar with the competition venue. Each step is an important part of preparing to perform.

Baseballers can often be seen walking the field a day or two before a game, getting a 'feel' for the stadium. They look at advertising signs and other structures, which they know will be there during the game. Thus while playing before a crowd of up to 50,000, the players can focus on the familiar structures and this helps them to feel comfortable and able to perform near to their best.

Going through this type of approach does not mean that they always win or achieve their aims. These successful athletes recognise that they

- won't perform at their optimum in every competition
- will sometimes be beaten
- will not be able to control the game for luck and other factors
- will sometimes do everything possible and still perform poorly

Despite these inevitable setbacks, successful athletes and teams continue to do the things they know will lead to success. Under these conditions they maintain poise, confidence and persistence.

In business, as in sport, you are not always able to choose the playing field. You can, however, create an environment around you that helps set you up with the best chance of succeeding. This might be as simple as spreading your papers out in a particular way before a presentation, or as complex as hiring a venue and having it constructed in a way to suit your needs. We pay particular attention to this aspect in our business athlete training programs in industry. Many organisations have found benefit in evaluating how well their physical environment and corporate culture are actually encouraging successful performance.

MAKE QUALITY THE STANDARD

Top athletes have a personal standard of quality against which they measure their performance. This does not mean that they exclude or ignore the results, but they do recognise that results can be misleading.

Top teams also set their own standards, which in some cases helps them to maintain superiority in a competition for many years.

Reggie Jackson, the famous American baseballer, was reported as saying even though he was one of the best batters in the world, he still struck out 7 times out of 10. Like most top performers, he knew that if he let himself believe that every strike-out was a bad strike-out then his confidence would quickly slump. Instead, he rated strike-outs from 'good strike-outs' that is, his performance was good, to 'poor strike-outs', where his technique or mental approach was astray. By looking more closely at the quality of his performance rather than just the outcome, he was able to maintain confidence and so give himself the most positive chance of hitting the next one.

GOOD STRIKE-OUT	POOR STRIKE-OUT
prepared well	undisciplined preparation
focused on ball	distracted
tracked ball	poor tracking of ball
well-timed swing	premeditated swing

> Top athletes recognise the quality of their own performance.

In the 1991 World Swimming Championships, Australian 1500 metre swimmer Kieren Perkins broke the world record by some seconds but still finished second. This is the type of situation which fully tests the capacity of the athlete to look at their *quality of performance* rather than simply the second place. Ideally, a swimmer gains a lot of confidence and satisfaction from performing so well and then sets his or her sights on improving still further, to possibly win the gold medal at the next opportunity.

In business, there is also considerable value in distinguishing between performance and outcome. Consider the situation of a personnel consulting firm that is commissioned by a major hotel to recruit an experienced catering manager.

Is the quality of the consulting firm's performance able to be measured by the quality of the person appointed to the position?

Perhaps it is, but what if the firm is also recruiting an administration manager for the same client? They follow the same thorough process for each position, but because of the standard of the applicants they are unable to locate a person of quality for the administration role.

Given this type of situation, in which the firm did everything possible to fill one of the positions and was unsuccessful, it is reasonable to consider the question, how else can the firm and the client measure performance?

Organisations that employ or retain the services of business athletes can benefit by recognising both **performance quality** and **performance outcome**. These are not one and the same thing, and when athletes in sport or business recognise this, they often place greater emphasis on quality at all stages of the work process, which leads to more consistent and reliable performance.

CONSISTENCY PRODUCES CONSISTENT RESULTS

The experience of top athletes in sport and business reveals that consistent performance is difficult to achieve when the focus is continually on end results.

Too much concern with the outcome actually distracts athletes from the performance itself. For example, prone rifle shooters seeking to shoot a perfect score of 600 find it difficult to maintain concentration over the last few shots of the match if they start thinking about the perfect score.

In business, an administrator who is only concerned with achieving the bottom line can miss many opportunities and therefore be less effective than someone who focuses on making the most of every opportunity to increase revenue or reduce expenditure.

> Winners do not let the outcome distract them from
> the task at hand.

WINNING ISN'T EVERYTHING

For many years it has been fashionable to use the phrase, 'Winning isn't everything, it's the only thing'. In the 1970s and 1980s, this theme was often used to fire-up sales people and others who attended motivational seminars and conferences. Unfortunately, the fall-out from this blinkered approach is still being felt. Banks who 'just wanted to win' chased bad-risk customers, retailers who 'just wanted to win' multiplied their overdrafts and manufacturers who 'just wanted to win' took short-cuts on quality.

For most business athletes winning is very important but it is only half the equation. If winning becomes the sole focus of your efforts, there is the real danger that you only do enough to beat your main competitor. What's wrong with that? Perhaps nothing, until someone else comes along with a new standard of quality which wipes both of you out of the market.

Being 'winning focused' means comparing your performance against someone else. While one way of measuring performance quality is as a comparison to others, there are, however, many other aspects to be considered.

A total focus on winning or losing is too simplistic and doesn't provide the information that athletes need to better their future performances.

The following diagram illustrates four dimensions of performance and outcome in a simple fashion.

A	B
won	lost
(good quality performance)	(good quality performance)
C	D
won	lost
(poor quality performance)	(poor quality performance)

Athletes are particularly challenged when faced by a loss where performance quality was good, as in quadrant B, or a win where performance quality was poor, as in quadrant C. To be able to recognise the quality of performance and not be misled by the outcome or result requires athletes to have a clear idea of the standards of performance that they expect of themselves.

Certainly, business athletes can benefit from objectively analysing the quality of their performance in the face of compliments, criticism and outward success or failure.

The importance of focusing on the quality of the process is dramatically illustrated in the following description by John Bertrand, skipper of *Australia II*, of the last few minutes of the final race for the America's Cup.

> We cannot even think of the result of this race, or what it will mean, because it is just too overwhelming. I know that none of us can even think for a fleeting second of what might happen if we should win, or if we should lose, or if we should make a mistake. All I must remember is to relax, relax, let it flow, let it flow.[6]

SET YOUR OWN LEVEL

Be prepared to set a level or a quality of performance and make that level something that you can achieve with effort.

Many athletes have set out to create their own brand of excellence in a way that has left the opposition floundering. Take inspiration from athletes such as hurdler Ed Moses, swimmer Mark Spitz, basketballer Michael Jordan, pole vaulter Sergei Bubka and tennis player Martina Navratilova. All of these world-class athletes did the basic things with style and, beyond that, set their own level which became the standard for others to follow.

Can you set a new standard in your chosen field?

Can you set a new standard of quality in any part of the process in your field?

Business athletes can set new levels of performance.

RECOGNISE ALL PLAYERS' CONTRIBUTION TO THE TEAM

Business organisations committed to business athlete training do not automatically assume that the best performer is the one who keeps the neatest books or makes the most sales. These outcome measures form only part of the judgement about the performance of team members.

Consider the sporting example of good football teams who may only have one or two people who score the goals. The best performers in these teams are often those who either get the ball to the players who score the goals or who stop the opposition from scoring. Good teams make sure that these players are also recognised.

Sometimes there are individuals within teams who don't fit the stereotype. Tom Peters and Robert Waterman in their book, *In Search of Excellence,*[7] described how the top performing organisations identified the performers ('product champions'), even when they didn't always fit into the comfortable stereotypes for that role.

How does your business team recognise the contributions of all members?

WATCH THE OFF-THE-BALL ACTIVITIES

A key factor in determining how well a football or basketball team performs is what individual players do when they haven't got the ball. This includes creating space, blocking or screening opposition players and communicating with team members.

Off-the-ball activities require players to be unselfish, disciplined, self-motivated and committed to a set of personal and team standards. A team committed to excellence in these off-the-ball activities is always going to be hard to beat.

A sure sign that a team is heading for the scrapheap is when standards in these areas fall down. It may take time to show on the scoreboard but sooner or later it will.

For a business athlete team the off-the-ball activities can include

- paying extra attention to product quality
- keeping the reception area tidy
- refusing to get involved in gossip
- filing items correctly
- doing something special for a customer
- ensuring that team members maintain physical health

Most off-the-ball activities don't appear in the job descriptions but sooner or later they are going to affect performance.

Can you describe ways in which your organisation could perform better in the off-the-ball activities? For example, paying extra attention to quality.

KNOW YOUR PERSONAL PERFORMANCE INDICATORS

When a group of management consultants completed business athlete training, they were each asked to list factors which might potentially measure the quality of their own personal performance. Their lists included the following items:

repeat business	referrals from existing clients
invitations to speak	keeping ahead of clients
colleagues of quality	meeting deadlines
acceptance of fees by clients	minimal complaints
being creative	maintaining a sense of humour
number of new clients	following through on plans
having a clear set of objectives	doing some physical exercise
number of published articles	enthusiasm

A group of sales professionals also produced a list including the following items:

number of calls	quality effort
prospecting activity	positive attitude
dress and grooming	tidy desk
assertiveness	using a time-management system
bouncing back from setbacks	energy level
making time for family	doing exercise
listening during interviews	complimenting other people
doing extra reading or study	calmness

Notice how these lists contain a combination of outcome and process indicators. This is important because one of the key aims of business athlete training is to assist clients to focus on and improve their work processes.

You can create your own list of personal performance indicators for your job and other important aspects of your life.

Consider the two examples given for each area:

YOUR JOB	YOUR LIFE
having a well-constructed diary system	working out in the gym three times a week
doing things methodically, not according to a whim	having a regular, quiet dinner at a restaurant with your spouse

USE A PERFORMANCE DIARY

Once a list of personal performance indicators has been developed, the next stage is to put these to practical use. Athletes do this by using performance diaries.

Performance diaries are laid out with a list of performance indicators that the athlete has found most closely determine their overall performance. For example, professional golfers may have identified key performance indicators including

- the consistent use of a pre-shot routine
- the number of greens hit in regulation number of strokes
- the ability to respond calmly to setbacks
- the percentage of saves from around the greens
- the accuracy of 'lag' putts

If these are the key factors that predict performance for these golfers then it is logical that they review these after each performance. This encourages the players to focus on high quality in each area and increases the chances of consistent, predictable performance.

Business athletes also use their own performance indicators to measure performance. They enter these in their regular diaries or use specially designed performance diaries which are provided as a part of business athlete training. A reduced version of the format of this diary appears opposite.

WEEKLY PERFORMANCE EVALUATION—MANAGER

Date: From   /   /   to   /   /

0 (not applicable) . . . 6 (highest)

								Comments
Planning and basic organisational skills	0	1	2	3	4	5	6	
Clearly defined goals	0	1	2	3	4	5	6	
Completion of key tasks	0	1	2	3	4	5	6	
Meeting deadlines	0	1	2	3	4	5	6	
Doing physical exercise	0	1	2	3	4	5	6	
Quality of time spent with children	0	1	2	3	4	5	6	
Quality of time spent with spouse	0	1	2	3	4	5	6	
Completing study program	0	1	2	3	4	5	6	
Maintaining a positive outlook	0	1	2	3	4	5	6	
Managing stress	0	1	2	3	4	5	6	

USE A PERSONAL SCOREBOARD
Almost all leading athletes avoid complicated systems, preferring those that are simple and effective. Most use some type of diary system, such as the one just described.

Why do they do this? In essence, what most look for is a 'scoreboard' which gives the most accurate picture of their performance. An example from football illustrates this point. On the surface it might seem that a football team can tell how they are performing by looking at the scoreboard, however, this can be quite misleading. For example, the scoreboard only tells us what has happened in the past and doesn't necessarily give a true picture of events as they are unfolding. The score on the scoreboard is also influenced by things like the quality of the opposition, umpiring, weather conditions, injuries and luck, all of which are outside the control of the players.

A more useful scoreboard is one which shows up-to-date information about the players' actual performance. On this scoreboard are things like amount of running when the team has possession, number of possessions, number of effective disposals, performance on 50-50 balls, tackles and so on.

Performance indicators or quality indicators for you, your job and your organisation are really your scoreboard. Apart from reviewing performance on a weekly basis, it is also useful to develop performance indicators for specific situations, such as an important presentation or a planning meeting.

> Athletes in sport and business develop their own scoreboard on which they record their personal performance indicators

USE 'TALKING DATA'

Athletes commonly work with a sport psychologist to seek assistance in improving concentration and self-confidence. The psychologist will usually begin by encouraging the athlete to make this request more specific. This means getting the athlete to describe specific behaviours which might result from improving concentration or confidence. For example, a tennis player instead of saying 'I want to improve my concentration' could start to make this more specific by saying 'I want to reduce the effect that worrying about winning or losing has on my performance.'

This second statement is getting closer to something the player and psychologist can use to plan a strategy and ways to measure its effectiveness. They might also add even greater specificity by rating the concentration level on a 1 (poor) to 10 (excellent) scale.

A challenge for business athletes is to convert ideas or opinions into data so that there is some consistency across their organisation or group. For example, rather than talking about an aspect of their performance as 'great', it is more useful to define this either in numerical terms—for example, 80 per cent—or comparative terms—such as better than x.

When you are discussing issues with other people, look for opportunities to convert ideas and opinions into hard data. This makes for less confusion, better communication and more effective information for managing performance.

Similarly, when assessing your own performance, look for opportunities to quantify the performance. Use rating scales, such as 0–100, to describe the quality of a presentation and get into the habit of comparing your own performances to see if there are differences that can be identified and worked on.

> Base ideas and opinions on specific data or on a reference scale wherever possible.

MATCH BEHAVIOUR TO GOALS

Another way in which athletes manage their performance is by looking for ways to transfer their longer-term goals into day-by-day and moment-by-moment behaviour. This ability to **match behaviour to main goals** is a simple and yet extremely effective system for individuals and teams.

At the Olympic Games this can be seen in its purest form, where athletes are totally focused on doing the things which they know from experience will lead to a peak performance. Under such conditions, the athletes make sacrifices, reject all types of interference such as the media and other athletes and limit themselves to their own patterns or rituals.

One of the simplest and most effective performance management techniques is to regularly ask yourself, 'How is this helping me to achieve my goals?' This does not mean that everything you do will fit into your goal program, but by being well organised and minimising the time spent on tasks that are irrelevant to goal achievement you are well on your way.

> Business athletes regularly ask themselves the question:
>   'How is this helping me to achieve my goals?'

PRACTISE DECISION MAKING
There are certain aspects of the decision-making processes used by athletes that can be employed by business athletes.

In field and racquet sports, athletes are regularly called upon to make decisions under pressure. These pressures include time restrictions, distractions and physical danger. One way in which the top performers can be distinguished from the lesser players is by the quality of their decision making. While some of this may be inherited, it has also been found that top performers take the time to plan responses to likely situations (contingency plans), then they develop back-up plans in case their main plan doesn't work. Finally, they practise both plans until they become automatic. This last point is vital because under pressure it will be the automatic or programmed behaviours which emerge.

A key role for coaches and sport psychologists is to ensure that athletes practise their decision-making skills under a range of conditions.

Decision training
Consider the example of a basketball coach who wants to train his players to make the correct decisions under competitive conditions.

Various situations and possible reactions will firstly be introduced in a non-stressful, educational way. This might include the use of videotapes, drawings on a board, written instructions and discussion.

Specific plays will then be set up at training and responses practised. The players will be encouraged to visualise or mentally rehearse their responses, possibly with the assistance of videotape feedback from training.

When these responses are learnt, the coach will introduce various pressures, including time restrictions and physical overload, to further strengthen the decision-making skills.

Finally, the skills will be used in competition, then reviewed, improved and then used again.

In industry and throughout the educational system, too often the training process finishes at the first or second step. This means that people learn skills, such as effective decision making or negotiation, but they are not then given the chance to practise these skills under difficult conditions.

Take the example of negotiation skills. Instead of going into a classroom and doing basic role plays, why not extend the training and require that participants go out into the 'real world' and practise their skills? This might mean doing something simple, like haggling over the price of an item in a retail store, or a more complex task such as convincing a taxi driver to drive you somewhere for half fare!

> Business athletes practise their skills so that they can be produced reliably in important situations.

CAPITALISE ON MOMENTUM
In the last two Rugby League Tests contested between Australia and New Zealand in Australia in 1991, the Australian team was so committed and developed such momentum that the All Blacks were virtually swept aside.

This experience of developing momentum is something that is common in all pursuits. Tennis players win point after point, sales representatives make a series of sales and corporations produce one successful product after another.

Any top athlete will tell you that when you are on a roll, keep it going. When your opposition is on a roll, however, do something to interrupt their momentum. Watch a tennis match between top-seeded players and notice how each attempts to control the pace and momentum of the game.

Business athletes also recognise that it is important to develop and maintain momentum. Organisations, teams and individuals all develop momentum.

Can you recognise when you and your team are on a roll?

Can you capitalise more on these situations?

Is there scope for you to (fairly) interrupt the momentum of a competitor?

BUSINESS ATHLETE AFFIRMATIONS
The following affirmations will help you to begin integrating the concepts from this chapter into your daily rituals. Use them regularly.

- 'I use action plans to bring my goals to life.'
- 'I set up myself and my team to succeed.'

- 'I evaluate my performance against my own professional and personal standards.'
- 'I use personal performance indicators to monitor my performance.'
- 'I focus on doing the little things well because these are the foundation on which my overall results are built.'
- 'I use my diary to plan and review performance.'
- 'I regularly manage my performance by asking, "How is this helping me to achieve my goal?"'
- 'I capitalise on momentum.'
- 'I ensure that my team recognises the off-the-ball activities.'

5

THE PERFORMANCE ZONE

> **Performing in the zone** means being inspired. It is
> total involvement in what you are doing: taking risks,
> doing things in an effortless and yet powerful way.
> The zone is total confidence in your ability to achieve
> all that you have visualised and prepared yourself to
> do.

Why do athletes sometimes produce exceptional performances? Why, for example, did American Bob Beamon, after almost fouling out in the qualifying rounds of the Mexico Olympics, produce a long jump that exceeded the existing world record by more than 53 cm and took 23 years to surpass?

Obviously, the higher altitude contributed to Beamon's performance but this certainly didn't explain the almost unbelievable distance he achieved.

Interestingly, most athletes at some stage of their careers report one or more experiences of performance that far exceed their typical level. These exceptional performances are accompanied by various physical and mental processes including

- high energy level
- focused concentration (absorbed in the task)
- effortlessness (a feeling of 'flow')
- optimism
- clear, rapid and accurate decision making

In business, similar experiences have been reported by people working in many different areas.

Can you recall a time when your performance flowed in a similar way? Perhaps it was a presentation which went just perfectly, a project where everything fell smoothly into place, or a day where every issue and decision seemed clear, logical and easy to resolve.

In this chapter we look at the fascinating topic of peak performance experiences and discuss how Olympic and professional athletes and teams actually set out to create these types of optimal performance experiences and how they can be applied to business performance.

WHAT IS 'THE ZONE'?
ACCESSING ALL OF YOUR ABILITIES
Athletes use the term **the zone** to describe the mental and physical state in which they perform at, or very close to, their best. For example, golfers who have experienced a 'hot streak' often comment afterwards that they felt inspired and thought they could attempt any shot. This is the zone, and for an athlete it is the most sought after experience in sport.

Olympic athletes do everything possible to get into their zone on the day of competition. They know from experience that this is the state of mind in which they can access all of their abilities, without any self-imposed negative influences.

For business athletes, performing in the zone means having access to a level of skill and performance that is higher than they typically experience.

What level of performance would you reach if you had access to all of your positive abilities, without any self-imposed negative influences?

INSPIRED
Performing in the zone means **inspiration**. It is total involvement in what you are doing: taking risks, doing things in an effortless and yet powerful way. The zone is total confidence in your ability to achieve all that you have visualised and prepared yourself to do.

Interestingly, top athletes often report that the absorption in the task is so complete that they have little recall of the detail of a zone performance. Downhill skiers for example, report being unable to remember going through many of the gates during their performance.

Many business athletes share similar experiences, such as

being so involved in delivering a speech that they are unable to remember the precise details afterwards; many are often surprised when they watch a videotape recording later.

Can you recall a time when you have been inspired in an activity in your chosen field of excellence?

CHANGES

The zone is characterised by **changes in perception**. Nigel Mansell, the British Formula One racing driver, was reported as saying that when he is in his zone, he can recognise the faces of individuals in the pit area as he speeds past at 200 miles per hour.[8]

Many athletes report other changes when in the zone, such as

- time seems to stand still
- opponents move more slowly
- thoughts are clearer
- less conscious effort

Business athletes performing in the zone report that they can

- think more clearly and logically
- visualise with amazing clarity and detail
- communicate more effectively
- do more in less time
- handle many tasks without losing focus on the main issues
- remain positive even when things are not going well
- establish instant empathy with clients

For athletes in sport and business there are also changes in other mental processes, such as an overall feeling of mental calmness. Many of our clients have spoken of being in a trance, aware of everything but unaffected by the distractions that might normally interfere with their performance.

Athletes also report physical changes, such as an absence of muscle tension and less fatigue than expected, even after best-ever performances. In business this translates into more energy and greater endurance to keep performing at a top level.

A ZONE, NOT A PEAK
OPTIMAL PERFORMANCE

The mental demands placed on the business athlete are remarkably similar to those experienced by the long distance runner. Both areas are endurance events requiring a consistently high level of performance over an extended period of time. Each therefore requires a purpose, persistence, self-discipline and a belief that the end goal is achievable.

One aspect of self-discipline evident in both distance running and in business is the requirement for performers to find an optimal level, or the pace that will allow them to reach their goal. This means that they perform at a level below their peak. For example, marathon runners can run faster in the first 10 kilometres but this detracts from their performance later. Similarly, in business you could push yourself to work flat-out on everything but might not last out the week.

This makes it more useful to think about optimal performance for the business athlete as a zone rather than a point or peak. This recognises that **consistency** and **persistence** rather than one explosive moment, are the keys to success. Similarly, athletes recognise that it is most productive to aim for optimal performance, rather than that one peak performance.

For the business athlete team, the experience of professional baseball players who might play in excess of 200 games per year is helpful. Players aim to be 'right' for each game, rather than reaching a peak. They find ways to create the energy or intensity that they need to be in their zone. Through business athlete training you can also learn to do the same.

> Business athletes recognise that business is an endurance event.

FINDING THE ZONE
REDUCE THE PRESSURE

Studies of top athletes across a range of sports have found that the winners are more often those athletes who perform with calmness and balance in even the toughest situations.

These athletes have developed an ability to reduce the pressure in a given situation and thereby find their zone.

It is also important to recognise that the top performers don't necessarily perform better under pressure than anyone else, instead they avoid letting the pressure build to the point where they lose control.

CALM MIND

For most athletes, performing in the zone is characterised by a relatively calm mind which is able to get the most performance from an efficient, active body.

Obviously the required level of 'psych-up' varies according to the nature of the sport. Sports such as weightlifting, field events in athletics and sprint canoeing require a high level of psych-up. Tennis, squash and basketball require players to be physically aroused but with a greater degree of control of mind and complex muscle movements, while at the lower end of the scale sports like bowls, shooting and archery demand calmness and self-control.

The same is true of business and professional activities. For example, the level of emotion or psych-up required to deliver a rousing address at a conference is much higher than that needed to perform delicate surgery. Rarely, however, are business performers trained to recognise the state of mental and physical intensity or psych-up which

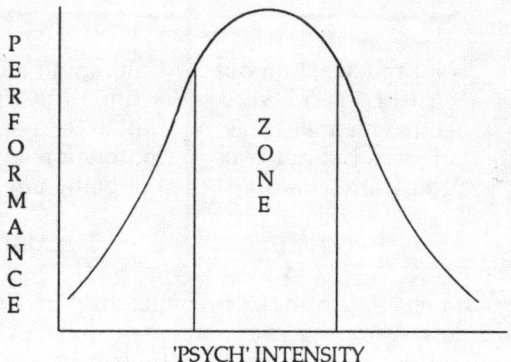

corresponds to their best performances.

Have you ever considered the best psych-up level for the main tasks in your job?

The common point, no matter whether you are playing a final at Wimbledon or finalising the corporate plan, is that there is a level of psych-up or intensity at which you perform at your best. This is illustrated on the previous page.

A MATTER OF STYLE

One way to further understand the concept of a performance zone is to consider that when you perform in the zone you will demonstrate a **mental style**—for example, calmness—and an **activity style**—active.   The four quadrants in the following diagram show this by illustrating four quite different states of mental style and activity style.

	Mental style	
	RUSHED	CALM
	A	**B**
ACTIVE	An over-active mind and plenty of activity (lots of short-term achievement, often followed by 'burn-out')	Lots of action and a calm mind (thinking calmly and clearly and getting full value for effort)
Activity Style	**C**	**D**
INACTIVE	Not much action but a rushed mind (very active mentally, lots of ideas but not really going anywhere)	Calm mind and no action (little drive, initiative or self-motivation: generally not going anywhere)
	RUSHED	CALM

The two dimensions from the previous diagram have been separated below. A star shows a common position for business athletes when they are performing in their zone.

Where do you believe your day-to-day style fits on each dimension?

Mental style

calm ......*... rushed

Activity style

active ......*... inactive

In what ways does your profile differ from the profile of the business athlete?

> A business athlete performing in the zone will demonstrate a mental style and a physical style.

FINDING YOUR ZONE

Athletes generally have an abundance of physical and mental energy. Much of the training undertaken by elite athletes is, in fact, designed to improve their energy systems. Athletes with a lot of physical energy can run further, jump higher and lift heavier weights than their competitors, while those with a good level of mental energy are better motivated, focused and more in control.

Athletes who have energy can perform with intensity. They know the level of intensity needed to perform at the top level in their chosen sport and they learn how to achieve this level.

The role that energy or intensity plays in performance cannot be over-estimated. In the following two sections we have used the term physical energy to refer to health and fitness issues and the term mental intensity to refer to the emotional and mental energy directed towards a task. For the business athlete, each is vital in establishing a foundation for winning in a competitive world.

> The business athlete recognises that physical energy and mental intensity are essential to achieving high performance.

PHYSICAL ENERGY

Athletes spend countless hours developing their bodies to peak physical condition. In business the obvious question is, is it important for business athletes to be in good physical condition?

The simple answer is both yes and no.

Firstly, no, they don't need to be as fit as an Olympic athlete. Secondly, however, as the demands on performers in business increase, yes, an appropriate level of physical health and fitness is essential to achieving a high level of consistent performance.

We have seen numerous program participants who have achieved marked increases in their at-work performance through participating in a health and fitness program. Health and fitness can mean developing

- flexibility
- muscle tone
- a desired weight
- cardiovascular fitness
- good dietary habits

To enhance your success profile, and as part of adopting the approach of the business athlete, we recommend that you arrange to undertake a complete fitness and health assessment. Further issues related to health and fitness are covered in chapter 12, 'Fit Body, Fit Mind'.

MENTAL INTENSITY

When athletes are performing in the zone they achieve the ideal level of mental intensity or psych level for their particular sport. Mental intensity is more difficult to define or measure than physical energy; however, performers learn to recognise the state of mind in which they perform at their best.

Given that there is a zone of optimal intensity, it stands to reason that there are also zones where there is too much or too little intensity. In sport, these are sometimes called zones of over- and under-arousal, while in business it is customary to refer to over-arousal as stress and under-arousal as low motivation.

Sources of stress at work can include

- conflicts with other people
- having too many tasks to complete
- routine tasks
- working in a position which doesn't suit
- striving to meet unrealistic deadlines

Often too much energy is used to resolve these issues, leaving little to devote to the key areas.

IN SEARCH OF YOUR ZONE

The most important first step towards finding your zone is to recognise when your energy or intensity level is too high or too low for optimal performance. Everyone has their own signs, which may show up as physical changes in the body, in their thinking and in their behaviour.

> Business athletes learn to recognise the signs that indicate their personal intensity level.

FIND YOUR PIN NUMBER

You probably have a PIN number for your bank account, however in this case we are referring to a different type of number.

Many athletes have found value in thinking about intensity on a scale from 1 to 10. The numbers from 1 to 4 represent those times when their personal intensity is too low. From 4 to 7 is the zone and from 7 to 10 indicates that their intensity is too high.

			P ersonal I ntensity N umber						
1	2	3	4	5	6	7	8	9	10
Very low				Z	O	N	E		Too high

At any time you can assess your own personal intensity and give it a number—your own PIN number.

ZONE SIGNS

The lists that follow illustrate some of the common signs of intensity levels being too high or too low. Some of the signs may apply to you and some, of course, may not. You might also find that some of the signs of being too intense, such as making errors or getting irritable, can also result from not being intense enough.

Intensity too low		Intensity too high	
PHYSICAL SIGNS 'How my body feels'		PHYSICAL SIGNS 'How my body feels'	
lethargic		shaking	
heavy		tight muscles	
out of condition		shallow breathing	
tired		'butterflies' in stomach	
slow reactions		light-headed	
sluggish		headaches	
THINKING SIGNS 'How I think'		THINKING SIGNS 'How I think'	
bored		anxious and uptight	
distracted		can't focus on one thing	
low creativity		worried about outcomes	
depressed		varying level of confidence	
uninterested		don't consider others' opinions	
slow thinking processes		impulsive decision making	
BEHAVIOURAL SIGNS 'What I do'		BEHAVIOURAL SIGNS 'What I do'	
move slowly		fidgety	
not much activity		lots of physical activity	
show little interest		smoke and/or eat more	
volunteer few new ideas		easily annoyed by other people	
not bothered with poor quality		frustrated if things don't work	
don't ask questions		get emotional	
don't measure performance		do too many little things	

WHY DOES INTENSITY GET TOO HIGH?

Athletes in sport and business face many pressures because they choose to put themselves into positions where they are challenged. For example, perhaps you have an event coming up which is really important, or you have just taken some major corporate restructuring decisions and are worried that they might not work out.

The list of reasons why people experience too much intensity is just about endless. Also, it is our attitude towards the events in our lives more than the events themselves that causes 'psych' levels to rise and fall. This, of course, explains why some people get very upset over little matters and yet stay calm and controlled in the face of a major disaster.

An important task in becoming a business athlete is to be attentive to the signs that tell you your intensity is not right and to then note what seems to trigger those feelings, thoughts or behaviours. For example, you might notice that you feel tense and irritable on the day before board meetings, or when you get less sleep than normal. Record these events in your diary and write three action plans for getting your intensity to a more appropriate level.

Here is an example to help you in developing your own action plans.

Intensity too high

CONFLICTING DEMANDS CAUSING ANXIETY (TOO MANY PROJECTS)

Action plans

1 Develop assertion to say no: attend a training course within the next two months.

2 Delegate more to personal assistant: meet to develop a specific plan.

3 Learn to use a personal computer: attend course next month.

WHY DOES INTENSITY GET TOO LOW?

Your intensity level can also get too low for many reasons. If you haven't had a holiday for a while, or if you've neglected to set a clear set of goals or objectives, then you can begin to feel lethargic and disinterested.

Just as the football player recognises when his intensity is falling, so too does the business athlete. Also, if you are managing others, one of your main roles is to be 'the playing coach'. This means keeping the team or organisation at an appropriate level of intensity.

Again, be alert to the signs that tell you your intensity level is too low, and take note of what seems to trigger those feelings, thoughts or behaviours. For example, you might notice that you feel bored and disinterested when you start the day late, or when working with people who show little drive or enthusiasm. Record these episodes in your diary and then write three action plans which will help you to lift your intensity in each situation.

Here is an example for low intensity.

Intensity too low

TIRED, NO DIRECTION OR MOTIVATION

Action plans

1 Within the next two weeks, develop a clearer set of priorities.
2 Set weekly performance targets.
3 Have a physical check-up and plan health and fitness accordingly.

WHAT'S NEXT?
In the next chapter you will learn how athletes practise a technique which helps them develop the mental calmness that goes with being in the zone.

BUSINESS ATHLETE AFFIRMATIONS
The following are the positive self-statements that will help you to begin integrating the concepts from this chapter into your daily rituals. Use them regularly.

- 'I recognise the signs which tell me that I am in my performance zone.'
- 'I maintain my performance as near to an optimum level as possible, because business is an endurance event, not a sprint.'

- 'I am aware of the signs that tell me my intensity is too high or too low.'
- 'Physical health and fitness are important to my overall performance.'
- 'I use my PIN number to help manage my intensity.'

6

ACTIVE CALMNESS

Business athletes generate active calmness to access their zone.

Athletes performing in the zone frequently report a feeling of calm concentration. Even in the more hectic sports, such as boxing and motor racing, there is this experience of mental calmness during peak performance.

We call this state of mind **active calmness** because it combines the two elements of calmness and activity. It is the mental style and activity style that is linked to high performance in competitive or challenging situations. Through regular practice, business athletes develop the skill of active calmness to the point where they can use their skills at a consistently high level.

Formula One racing driver Nigel Mansell hinted at this skill during a segment on British television. He told the story of batting against a baseball pitching machine. As the ball was released at 150 km/h, he slowed it down in his mind to 50 km/h and made 25 hits out of 25 attempts.[9] This is an excellent example of how an athlete who has trained himself over many years to retain a calm focus of concentration can reduce the perception of speed. One of the differences between the top Formula One drivers and those a level below may well be this ability to create a **zone performance** in which the perception of speed is reduced and control of the car enhanced through generating active calmness.

In business, the concept of active calmness contrasts with the busy workaholic image which in the past so typified many organisations. Recently, companies have begun to count the cost of such stereotypes in high turnover, stress levels, illness, lack of creative drive and falls in productivity. Too many business performers have acted like sprint cyclists when, in fact, the event was more like a tour being contested over hundreds of kilometres. Just like the cyclist who surges to the lead early in a long race, they gain some short-term recognition but are quickly overtaken by the leading bunch and are burnt out long before the race concludes.

ENTERING THE ZONE
Business athletes find that they enter the zone more often when in a state of active calmness or when they have recently experienced sessions or periods of calmness.

Recent developments have shown that athletes can be trained to develop the skill of active calmness in the same methodical fashion that they learn their sporting skills. Athletes in most countries now undertake this type of training as part of their build-up to major competitions. Eastern European countries, in particular, have used extensively a form of active calmness training called autogenic training, which involves learning to control tension and temperature in specific muscle groups.[10] More recently, Western athletes have turned to meditation, t'ai chi, hypnosis, floatation, total relaxation and other related techniques in the search for ways to develop active calmness.

Tennis player Arthur Ashe has also been widely reported as crediting the use of a brief calming activity between games with helping him to win the Wimbledon tennis championships. Australian Olympic gold medallist Debbie Flintoff-King also credited a form of mental calmness training with helping her to achieve an Olympic gold medal in Seoul in 1988.[11]

Active calmness is essential to the business athlete because it combines aspects of calmness and concentration that are key factors associated with high level performance.

If you recall your own best performances you might find that many of these were associated with focused concentration and an inner sense of calmness and control.

The following sections explain more about this important skill and describe a training process which you can follow to learn and develop the skill.

ACQUIRING THE SKILL OF ACTIVE CALMNESS

During business athlete training conducted in industry, participants are trained in the skill of active calmness through three quite distinct yet interrelated phases. These are explained briefly below and training instructions then follow.

PHASE 1 EXPERIENCING CALMNESS

The aim of this phase is to develop a greater level of calmness than you normally experience. This helps to establish a type of reference point, that is, a low PIN number, which becomes important when calmness is required in a performance.

We usually structure activities for our clients so that they experiment with various types of experiences and in that way learn which is most effective for them. Amongst the techniques used are muscle tension reduction (MTR), meditation, floatation and hypnosis.

Many of our international athletes use a combination of floatation and meditation because this helps them to recover both physically and mentally from training. Interestingly, an increasing number of our business athlete clients are using a similar approach.

PHASE 2 LEARNING TO DEVELOP CALMNESS

Once you have experienced calmness, the next stage is to learn how to develop physical and mental calmness on a more regular basis. This can be achieved through an activity that reduces muscle tension and then focuses, clears and quietens the mind. To be successful it requires a quiet, distraction-free environment. This method is only one of the techniques generally covered in a 12-month corporate business athlete training program, however it is one that has been widely acclaimed by business and sporting athletes.

You will require daily training of between 14 and 21 days to develop the basic level of calmness needed to move on to the next phase. To achieve full, ongoing benefits, the training needs to be continued on a regular basis as a part of daily routines. In this respect, many athletes include a daily 20–30 minute session of calmness in their training program.

PHASE 3 DEVELOPING ACTIVE CALMNESS

The key to active calmness is to be able to transfer the benefits of calmness learnt in the quiet, distraction-free environment into competitive or challenging situations. For athletes such as downhill skiers, this means maintaining an inner feeling of calmness when racing at over 100 km/h down a slalom course.

The business equivalent of the downhill are all of those times when everything seems to be speeding up, where the demands on you seem to outstrip your resources and where calmness will help you to use your skills to the fullest.

The main tools are a controlled breathing technique and a continued emphasis on focusing your concentration on things which can be controlled. By using the correct breathing technique and building this into daily rituals, you can learn to tap into feelings of mental calmness under all conditions.

TRAINING INSTRUCTIONS

The instructions below describe a training process. It is essential to the success of that process that you follow each step. Furthermore, it is the experience of calmness and active calmness which we are seeking, not just an understanding of the concept.

SELECT A REGULAR TIME AND PLACE

Find a place that matches the state of mind and body for which you are training. This is a place that is quiet, distraction-free, comfortable and warm. Plan a time each day when you will complete your training. It is best to allow 20–30 minutes for at least one, and no more than two, sessions per day. Try to avoid times straight after meals, as digestion affects the calming process, or when you are very tired.

PREPARE FOR CALMNESS

Calmness is best learnt when wearing loose-fitting clothes and no shoes, although loose slippers are all right. It can also be helpful to wash your hands and face with cool water prior to taking up your position because this helps to clear away feelings of tiredness.

Sit in a comfortable chair and adopt a posture which is symmetrical. This means a comfortable, straight back, with hands clasped loosely in the lap and feet flat on the floor about shoulder width apart. Avoid slouching or leaning forward.

MUSCLE TENSION REDUCTION (MTR)

Muscle tension reduction (MTR) training is designed to help you experience less tension throughout your body. MTR training is a precursor to achieving mental calmness.

As we mentioned earlier in this chapter, our usual approach is to introduce clients to a range of calming experiences before commencing the specific training. One of these options is MTR, and we have included it in this book because it is a technique that requires no equipment or direct training from a psychologist.

MTR is easy to use and effective. It involves dividing the body into six zones and systematically stretching, loosening and then releasing tension in the muscle groups in that zone.

The six general zones, listed in the order in which they are attended to, are

- hands and arms
- shoulders and upper back
- chest, stomach and abdomen
- lower back and hips
- legs and feet
- scalp, face and neck

Assume a seated position and allocate between 2 and 4 minutes for each zone, during which time you go through a three-step process.

1. **stretch the muscles** to a comfortable extent.
2. **loosen the muscles** by moving them around and gently tightening and loosening them.
3. **release tension** and let the muscles hang limply.

Repeat this activity a few times with each muscle group and you will begin to notice less tension in the muscles. It can also be helpful to coordinate the activity with the rhythm of your breathing so that you release the breath as you release the muscle tension. You may have your eyes open or closed, depending on which gives the better effect.

When you have worked through all six zones, take a few

more minutes to sit quietly before going about your work or other activities.

Continue with MTR for approximately one week, or until you experience a genuine feeling of reduced tension in the muscles. When you reach this point, go on to the next stage.

CALMNESS TRAINING

Calmness training begins with six minutes of MTR during which time you take approximately one minute per body zone to stretch, loosen and release tension.

The remainder of this stage is completed with your eyes open, focusing on an object placed directly in front of your vision. While you may wish to close your eyes, it is important not to. The transfer of calmness skills from this non-stressful situation to a performance situation will be most effective when you have learnt the skill with your eyes open.

The point of focus is entirely your choice. Many people find that a candle is an ideal medium in a still room, however other focal points can include dots on the wall, photographs and any other item or point which allows you to maintain a neutral gaze.

There are two main components to calmness training: developing the skill of concentration and using the correct breathing method. These are developed together.

BREATHING AND CALMNESS

Focus your gaze onto the chosen item or point. Breathe in slowly, smoothly and quietly, giving as little interruption to your mind and body as possible. Let the air push out your lower stomach and abdomen. Visualise that you are breathing in calmness.

Breathe out even slower. Imagine that tension is leaving your body with each breath. When you have exhaled, focus on the stillness which can occur between one breath and another.

It may take quite a few sessions for you to become aware of the stillness; however, it is this feeling you are looking to capture so perseverance will be rewarded. Do not force it; simply repeat the same slow, effortless, natural abdominal breathing pattern over and over. Make sure that you do not wait too long between breaths or breathe in too slowly as this will just restrict oxygen and reduce the value of the whole activity.

The following diagram highlights the simplicity of the process.

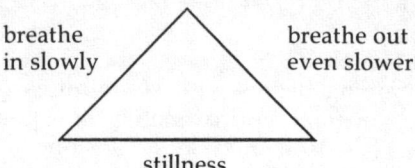

breathe
in slowly

breathe out
even slower

stillness

Mental calmness is achieved through the combination of

- focusing on the chosen point or object
- awareness of the stillness between breaths
- an associated clearing of the mind

During the whole activity, focus your attention on the chosen object and develop the feeling that there is nothing but the feeling of stillness and the point on which you are focusing.

Your mind will probably not want to clear itself of all thoughts apart from the stillness and the focal point. This is quite natural and is reported by virtually all sportspeople and business athletes when they begin training. Let your response to intrusive thoughts be no more than to just refocus on your breathing, on stillness and the focal point.

The main barrier

The main barrier for most trainees is to accept that it takes time to achieve active calmness and that their minds will seem at times to be quite opposed to the process. This is fine: remember that your mind is accustomed to being active and it is certainly not used to the level of calmness that can occur during this training. Be satisfied if at any time during the training, even if only for a moment, you experience the feeling of stillness.

There are various adaptations to this process. One you might find helpful is to choose a word or words to say quietly to yourself as you breathe out. This is like a mantra used during meditation, and any word that has meaning for you can be helpful. Some which have been used by business athletes include 'calm', 'relax', 'still' and 'power'. Reciting a particular word as you breathe out may help you to focus your concentration, and increase the feelings of calmness.

Some people find that quiet, peaceful music helps them to achieve calmness. Experiment with this.

REACHING THE DESIRED STATE OF CALMNESS
Most trainees ask how they will know when they have reached the level of calmness required. The only answer is that you will know: the feeling of calmness will be quite recognisable.

At best, during most calming sessions you will experience only a few minutes of real calmness. At the beginning of your training program, it will take time to reach the level which you require, and the calmness will tend to flow at different depths depending on many factors, including the pressures in your life.

CALMNESS IN AN ACTIVE ENVIRONMENT
The second phase does not usually begin on a specific day but evolves gradually. This means that as you get better at achieving calmness in the quiet, distraction-free environment, so you will be inclined to use the skills in more challenging situations. Also, the calmness experienced during these sessions will have a carry-over effect into daily activities. For example, many athletes meditate daily and report that this helps them to remain calmer and to focus better under tough competitive conditions.

The key to maintaining active calmness in challenging situations is to condition yourself to apply the breathing technique learnt earlier to many different situations. Athletes do this by building the breathing technique into their pre-performance rituals. Watch top tennis players before they serve, or divers before taking up their position on the board. They are using a simple tool for setting themselves closer to their zone.

BUILD CALMING INTO YOUR RITUAL
Conditioning in the use of the breathing technique begins by identifying situations that occur every day. These might include waiting at traffic lights, answering the telephone or

listening to others talk. Once these situations are identified, it is then up to you to make a point of focusing on your breathing and creating a moment or two of calmness. The breathing technique emphasises slow, abdominal breathing.

It is essential that you build calming into your rituals because these are the bridges between calmness in a quiet, distraction-free environment and active calmness in performance.

If calming is not built into the rituals, it will not occur automatically under the conditions when it is needed most. Be like the top athletes who automatically take a calming breath before shooting, throwing, serving, jumping and starting an event.

MAKE A LIST OF TIMES WHEN CALMING IS NEEDED
The final phase is to identify those situations where calming could be useful. These will include those situations where you feel that you might be too psyched up or too intense, together with those where you really want to perform well.

Make a list of these situations in your diary and note also the key things you need to concentrate or focus on. Some examples from sport, work and other activities are given to illustrate how calmness can be followed by a focusing of attention.

SPORT	WHEN TO USE CALMING	WHAT TO FOCUS ON
motor racing	immediately prior to the start of the race	the starter's signal
football	prior to kicking for goal	alignment and 'feel'
baseball	a batter stepping up to the plate	the pitcher's movements
golf	before addressing the ball	alignment, swing

NON-SPORT ACTIVITY	WHEN TO USE CALMING	WHAT TO FOCUS ON
work	when the phone rings	listening to caller
home	when the children are arguing	resolving the 'stoush' quietly
work	when a staff member produces poor work	the specific areas that need to be improved
driving a car	when late for an important meeting	calmness, driving safely
work	just before beginning a presentation	calmness, and the first point or two in the presentation

ONGOING TRAINING
To gain the full benefits from active calmness training continue to practise both the calming and active calmness skills on a daily basis.

As you start to reap the benefits you will see that this is not an imposition but rather an experience which you will come to look forward to each and every day. Many athletes swear by the value of calmness training and an increasing number of business people are realising the link between calmness and performance.

Other skills, such as visualisation and positive self-instruction, can also add to the benefits gained from active calmness and these are covered in later chapters.

> Active calmness is a key performance skill because it combines concentration and calming. These are two of the major characteristics identified with performing in the zone.

ACTIVE CALMNESS CHECKLIST
The points below summarise the key steps involved in active calmness training.

- a quiet, distraction-free environment
- 20–30 minutes each day at a regular time
- loose-fitting clothes
- wash hands and face with cool water
- a comfortable chair
- symmetrical posture
- stretch, loosen and release muscles in each zone
- choose a point of focus; for example, a candle
- slow, abdominal breathing
- stillness between breaths
- consciously release tension in muscles
- calm the mind; focus on stillness
- breathe in calmness, breathe out negative feelings
- do *not* be concerned over unwanted thoughts
- use a word on exhaling, for example, 'calm'
- music can be helpful
- imagery can be helpful, for example, visualise a mountain
- let active calmness evolve
- use rituals as bridges to link calmness with performance

OTHER METHODS OF ACHIEVING ACTIVE CALMNESS
The ability to achieve physical and mental calmness is closely linked to optimal performance. Business athletes have much to gain from learning and practising one or more methods of calming as well as following an appropriate physical health and fitness program.

There are many other forms of calmness training available. Some of those that are incorporated into business athlete training programs include the following.

FLOATATION TANKS
These are now readily accessible in most major cities. They are rather like a bath with a curved lid on it, containing a small amount of very salty water. The experience of calmness is achieved through floating in the salt water in an environment free from distractions such as light and noise.

Floatation therapy is now widely used by people from all walks of life. These tanks are used at Institutes of Sport for athletes to recover from intense training and to prepare for future competitions. Business athletes can also experience the tremendous benefits that can flow from a regular floatation session. Forward-thinking corporations are already setting up floatation centres within their own offices so that their business athletes can benefit from regular floating.

YOGA AND T'AI CHI

Both of these are forms of exercise that incorporate methods for calming the mind and body. Most people learn the techniques in classes and then build these activities into their everyday routines.

Training in yoga also incorporates many breathing techniques and these can be valuable for business athletes.

MEDITATION

Meditation is the general term for a range of techniques, some of which are similar to the mental calmness activity you completed in this chapter.

Meditation combines relaxed concentration with progressive relaxation of the mind and body. While meditation has often been associated with religious or spiritual beliefs, it is now quite widely taught without this emphasis.

Many athletes use meditation as a way of finding mental and physical calmness, and a number of major organisations have introduced forms of meditation training for their staff. Business athletes who choose to complete one or two meditation sessions per day commonly report marked reductions in stress and improvement in their performance.

SELF-HYPNOSIS

Self-hypnosis is an excellent calming technique taught by qualified psychologists. It provides for relatively quick and efficient calming. Interestingly, many experts equate the feelings of absorption in the task experienced when in the zone with the experience of hypnosis. Both feature total concentration.

Self-hypnosis is also used to enhance the value of visualisation and to introduce suggestions about future performance.

MASSAGE
Most athletes make use of massage on a regular basis. Massage relieves muscle tension and helps them manage the challenge of intense training and competition.

Business athletes can also gain considerable benefits from a regular therapeutic massage carried out by a qualified masseur.

BUSINESS ATHLETE AFFIRMATIONS
Below are some positive self-statements to help you begin integrating the concepts from this chapter into your daily rituals. Use them regularly.

- 'I see active calmness as helping me to create and sustain a consistently high level of performance.'
- 'I regularly practise the skill of active calmness.'
- 'I am getting better and better at developing and maintaining active calmness.'
- 'I encourage my team members to develop active calmness.'

7

A WINNING FOCUS

> Business athletes control what can be controlled and
> minimise the distracting effects of what cannot be
> controlled.

The 1976 Montreal Olympics produced one of the most
astonishing performances in Olympic history. Coming to the
final exercise in the men's team gymnastics competition, the
Japanese team were placed to win a medal. Sadly, one of
their team had broken his leg in a fall earlier and unless
this gymnast could perform at his best, their medal chance
would be gone. The last exercise was the rings, an activity
the gymnast could possibly complete with discomfort, except
for the dismount which required a 3-metre-high somersault
followed by a landing on both feet, in which the position
had to be held stable.

The crowd watched in awe as the gymnast worked through
the routine, showing no signs of the broken leg. Then, as
every person in the stadium held their breath, the gymnast
released his grip of the rings, flew high into the air, completed
the somersault and landed, holding his position long enough
for a successful dismount. Only then did he allow his focus
of concentration to acknowledge the pain of the broken leg.

This remarkable story vividly highlights the capacity of
top athletes to focus their concentration onto the task at hand,
even under the most trying conditions. Top athletes consider
focusing to be a key performance skill that needs to be
practised until they can do it successfully under all types
of conditions.

Performance quality is very closely linked to the capacity
of athletes to focus their concentration in the way demanded

by their sport. While the importance of focusing is quite evident in sport, it is not so readily appreciated in business.

In this chapter we introduce the concept of focusing and show how business athletes add to their performance quality by improving this vital skill.

TYPES OF FOCUS

While most top athletes have their own distinctive style of concentration, each sport does place certain restrictions or requirements on the competitors. Similarly, in business there are many different styles of concentration, although certain jobs require a certain focusing style.

In sport and business it is helpful to consider the skill of focusing as being divided into three broad types or directions:

1. Target focus
2. Field focus
3. Self focus

1. TARGET FOCUS
What is target focus?
Most sports require athletes to fine-tune their focus, even if only for a moment. Focus can be on a point; for example, a ball or an opponent, or on a target of some type. Shooting is the most obvious example of target focus. Athletes in sports requiring a high degree of target focus need to be skilled at maintaining focus in the face of many potential distractions such as noise, movement or thoughts about the score.

Many business tasks require a target focus. Most writing, statistical and computing tasks are like this because they require the person to focus on the task and to ignore other things. Business athletes with a good target focus can

- ignore distractions
- refocus after interruptions
- give their full attention to one task at a time
- do detailed work under pressure

Can target focusing be done too much?
Too much target focus can lead to missing things and taking too narrow a view of what is happening. Business executives who are too target focused can be out of touch with their staff, customers or competitors.

To what extent does your job require a target focus?
How well do you target focus?

How can target focus be improved?
If your performance depends upon the capacity to target focus and you identify a need to improve this skill, there are various ways to make an improvement. Some techniques include:

- being aware of the nature of distractions
- developing a strategy for managing those distractions
- practising active calmness
- setting specific, short-term goals
- dividing tasks into small segments (see chapter 8)

2. FIELD FOCUS
What is field focus?
Team sports such as football, lacrosse, basketball and volleyball require players not only to target focus on the ball but also to be very aware of their surroundings. Really good players seem to have a sixth sense about where their opponents and team members are, and this is an example of field focus.

In business, field focus includes both operational and strategic aspects. An example of **operational field focus** is the control room of a chemical plant where controllers continually scan instrument display panels, searching for signs which suggest that the plant is not operating according to plan. An example of **strategic field focus** is the chief executive officer of a group of companies who oversees the operations of each company and also looks for opportunities to add to the group. In each case, the ability to scan, take in and filter information is critical.

Business athletes with good field focus

- know what is happening around them
- rarely get caught unaware
- continually look for opportunities
- know what their staff are doing
- watch how other people act

Can field focusing be done too much?
Too much field focus can lead to a lack of attention to detail in a task or project.

To what extent does your job require a field focus?
How effectively do you field focus?

How can field focus be improved?
If your performance requires the capacity to field focus and you identify a need to improve in this area, there are various ways to make an improvement. Some ideas include

- being more aware of your environment
- having a strategic plan; for example, a flow diagram or a checklist
- practising tasks that require field focus
- modelling people who are proficient in this area

3. SELF FOCUS
What is self focus?
In sports such as gymnastics and diving, the competitors spend most of their time focusing on their own body position and movement. This is called self focus.

Self focus in business is also considered to include activities that are mind-centred. For example, architects, artists, writers and creative staff in advertising agencies all spend a significant time in self focus.
Can self focusing be done too much?
Too much self focus can lead to what athletes call 'paralysis by analysis'. This occurs where athletes pay so much attention to what they are doing that the skill breaks down. For example, golfers who think too much about the components of their swing find that the total swing completely freezes.

Business athletes who are too self focused can lose sight of the context of real world. This can be seen at times when ideas are impractical or take an extremely long time to be developed. Businesses can also become too self focused— the endless flow of internal memos in some organisations is an example of this phenomenon. In effect, these businesses do business with themselves instead of providing exceptional customer service.

Business athletes who are good at self focusing

- are self aware
- can work by themselves
- often like to develop ideas and strategies

To what extent does your job require a self focus?
How well do you self focus?

How can self focus be improved?
Increasing self focus is largely a case of increasing self-awareness. This can be achieved through a detailed post-performance review. Athletes do this by reviewing the actual thought processes that occurred during a performance, while public speakers watch videotapes of their performance and plan ways to improve and monitor their voice projection and gestures.

> Business athletes recognise that each work task requires a specific type or combination of focus.

PERFORMANCE FOCUSING

A professional tennis player is playing the game of his life against one of the top players in the world. Leading 30–15 and 5–2 in the final set, the player drives a crisp forehand down the line and a loud call of 'Out!' comes from the linesperson in the far corner. The player is aghast and immediately protests to the umpire, who steadfastly refuses to overrule the call. Over the next 20 minutes the player loses five consecutive games and the match is over.

This all-too-common scenario shows how something outside the control of the player, such as a line call, leads to an emotional upset, a loss of focus and ultimately a slump in performance.

No matter whether you are playing tennis, selling advertising space or managing a major corporation there will always be:

- factors over which you have, or can achieve, **total control**.
- factors over which you can assert a **controlling influence**.
- factors over which you have **no control**.

Top athletes in sport and business are acutely aware of the level of control they have over each factor that might influence their performance.

With a little thought you will be able to identify and

categorise those aspects in your work and general lifestyle which are

- controllable
- partly or possibly controllable
- not controllable

The following table illustrates examples from sport, business and general lifestyle areas. If you are part of a team, then also consider those aspects that are controllable or uncontrollable for your team.

CONTROLLABLE

SPORT	BUSINESS	GENERAL LIFESTYLE
effort	weekly plan	goals
goals	stock levels	fitness activities
basic skills (sport specific)	choice of targets	diet
planning strategies	negotiating position	quality of family time
how I choose to react	focus of concentration	time spent with friends
energy level	response to competition	social activities
focus of concentration	organisation structure	reading habits
self-discipline	formatting of information	time spent watching television
attitude	meeting agenda	study/self-development

PARTLY CONTROLLABLE

SPORT	BUSINESS	GENERAL LIFESTYLE
team patterns	quality of staff	spouse
coaching style	staff behaviour	children
the future	equipment	time available to be at home
opponents in some sports	transport costs	housing
teammates' performance	other departments/ sections	health
umpire's interpretation	the future	standard of living

NOT CONTROLLABLE

SPORT	BUSINESS	GENERAL LIFESTYLE
weather	the economy	cost of living
facilities at competition site	policies of competitors	changes in community values
rules	council regulations	weather
umpire's decisions	competitors' actions	people
past mistakes and successes	petrol price	traffic congestion
expectations of other people	weather	location of shops
approval of other people	union demands	interest rates
opponent's reactions	trade wars	content of television programs

A business athlete performing in the zone automatically (subconsciously) focuses towards those aspects that can be controlled. Aspects which can't be controlled are either dealt with in the least intrusive way or ignored.

In order to do this effectively business athletes learn to

- Manage the controllables
- Filter the distractions
- Use damage control

1. MANAGE THE CONTROLLABLES
Poor performance can often be traced to failing to manage the controllables. Every time that we fail to attend to a controllable, we potentially concede something that might impinge on quality. This applies equally to the tennis player who doesn't cover the net as it does to the manager who fails to read the maintenance schedule.

The reliable, consistent performance achieved by business athletes is built on the principle of making sure of the controllables. One of the effects of this is that they are less reliant on good fortune. This can be equated with the golfer who takes time to align his feet and club correctly before every shot. This can save one or two shots during a round and might be enough to offset the inevitable one or two extra strokes that result from unlucky bounces or putts which do not drop.

> Business athletes do not concede the controllables.

2. FILTER THE DISTRACTIONS

One of the reasons Olympic teams employ performance psychologists is that there are more potential distractions such as media, travel, the village and expectations at the Olympics than at any other competition. Psychologists assist the coaches and athletes to develop strategies for managing their environment in a way that minimises the negative effects.

Business athletes also arrange and manage their working environment in a way that minimises the negative influence of distractions. This can include scheduling difficult tasks at less busy times of the day, delegating, having calls screened and simply saying no to requests.

Some of the distractions identified by business athletes include

- poor staff
- poor early results during a long-term project
- telephone calls and unwanted visitors
- economic conditions
- ill-health
- tight deadline

What are some of the key distractions that you face in your chosen field?

> Business athletes are skilled at filtering the potentially damaging effects of distractions.

3. USE DAMAGE CONTROL

It is quite unrealistic to expect athletes in sport or business to perform consistently over a long period without having their performance interrupted, at least at some stage, by a distraction that is uncontrollable.

In these situations, the aim of most athletes is to minimise the effect. For example, a business athlete cannot ignore the effects of a recession but can minimise the distracting effects through taking specific action. Similarly, an athlete can minimise the distracting effects of well-intentioned supporters before an important event by finding a quiet spot away from the distractions.

If you find yourself getting upset about the economy, another person's behaviour, or something else which you can't control, then ask yourself, 'Can I really do anything about it?'

If the answer is no, then follow the lead of top athletes who use the skill of active calmness to stay focused on the things they can control.

TWO TIPS FOR BETTER FOCUSING
Two other techniques that athletes use to develop and maintain a winning focus are
  1. doing the little things brilliantly
  2. doing the scouting

1. DO THE LITTLE THINGS BRILLIANTLY
Top athletes limit the effect of factors such as weather, referees and other people on their performances. One way they do this is by doing the little things brilliantly.

These little things include the tasks that often require effort but do not produce immediate results. Examples include working off-the-ball in basketball, maintaining detailed dossiers on opponents or keeping a performance diary. Leading athletes know that attention to these factors gives them an edge over those opponents who leave these things to chance.

A sure sign that a sporting or business team or individual is in trouble is when the little things start to be ignored or treated haphazardly. The effects usually aren't evident immediately, however they soon start to show on the scoreboard.

For business athletes the little things can include

• having a daily plan
• keeping up-to-date with paper work
• doing some physical activity
• arriving on time for meetings
• always being courteous to customers or clients
• supporting team members

The little things are the foundation on which success is built. They provide a focus for attention and effort. By focusing on performance quality at this level the potential for consistent, reliable, high quality performance is immediately enhanced.

> Business athletes recognise the importance of the little things and attend to them with the same care and quality that is devoted to tasks of obviously major importance.

What little things are the foundation of your work performance?

2. DO THE SCOUTING

Olympic and professional athletes and teams learn from experience that if they do not focus on making sure of the controllables, then they rely too heavily on the areas that they can only partially influence. In a highly competitive or difficult situation, this can be fatal to performance.

One aspect that really separates the top coaches and athletes from the level below is the amount and quality of scouting they do. Scouting means finding out about your opposition, the playing conditions and any other factors that might influence performance.

The following examples from sport and business demonstrate vividly the effect of not doing this thoroughly.

- A boxer neglected to watch all videotapes of his opponent and was knocked out by a surprise punch in the third round.
- A lacrosse team didn't watch their main opponents play the weakest team. In the final they were destroyed by a play which their opponents had practised in that game.
- A shooter didn't double-check competition times, arrived too late for 'sighters' and missed an almost certain Olympic medal.
- A secretary didn't check details on an envelope containing an important proposal. The error was not identified until after the deadline for submissions. The proposal would have been accepted had it arrived on time.
- A consulting firm tried to minimise costs on administrative support for consultants and ultimately lost all consulting staff within an 18-month period.

- A staff member of a finance organisation disposed of confidential client information in a box that was later discovered at a rubbish dump and forwarded to the media.

Business athletes recognise the importance of maintaining focus on the 'main game'. Obviously the fewer surprises that occur along the way the better their focus will be and therefore the better their performance. One of the keys to minimising the surprises is thorough scouting.

> Business athletes do their homework and then focus on doing the little things brilliantly.

BUSINESS ATHLETE AFFIRMATIONS
The following affirmations are used in business athlete training programs in industry. We have included them to help you to begin integrating the concepts from this chapter into your daily rituals. Use them regularly.

- 'I recognise the main types of focus required in my profession.'
- 'I focus my concentration in the best way to suit each task that I undertake.'
- 'I am aware of the level of control I have over the many factors that influence my performance.'
- 'I focus on controlling the things over which I have control and minimise the distracting effects of those things over which I have no control.'
- 'I control as many aspects of my performance as possible.'
- 'I do the little things brilliantly.'

8

FOUR PERFORMANCE TOOLS

> Business athletes select personal targets and develop
> a game plan for achieving these targets.

All athletes strive to develop and maintain control over their performance; only a few, however, achieve the level of control which they desire. This select group almost invariably uses four performance tools.

1. Personal targets
2. A game plan
3. Performance rituals
4. Task splitting

Each tool is easy to use; however, to ensure their reliability under all conditions, leading athletes take every opportunity to practise and fine-tune the use of these tools.

In this chapter we detail each of the performance tools and show how business athletes use them to control their own performance.

PERSONAL TARGETS

Athletes in sport and business perform better when they have clear daily and weekly targets. These short-term targets or goals are part of the foundation on which they build their performance. They use each target to enhance motivation and to provide a focus for effort.

The most effective personal targets are those that are measurable, such as race time, number of goals, premium income and performance against budget. Recent research has also shown that those athletes who set the most accurate personal targets gain the greatest benefits.[12] These include

- improved performance
- greater self-confidence
- better concentration
- greater satisfaction and enjoyment
- less stress

Business athletes convert corporate targets into personal targets and set these at realistic levels. They measure many aspects of their performance and use these measures to create additional targets. They take responsibility for their own consistent improvement by setting progressively more challenging targets.

In what ways can you convert corporate targets into your own personal daily or weekly targets?

Organisations committed to the business athlete approach develop an environment in which personal targets are rewarded and emphasis is placed on consistent improvement of each individual and team.

Business athletes regularly set accurate personal targets.

A GAME PLAN

Athletes who want to win or play well and who don't take the time to develop a game plan risk losing control of performance in competition. The game plan is the framework around which athletes build their performance. The best athletes and coaches develop their game plans and practise them until they become second nature. An excellent example is the set plays used by professional basketball teams. These plays are choreographed and rehearsed until every player can produce a given play under even the most intense pressure.

Leading athletes also develop a 'Plan B'. This is the back-up competition plan and they practise it just as much as the main plan. Interestingly, one of the noticeable differences between top athletes and teams when compared with the level below is in the attention they pay to rehearsing a game plan and a back-up plan.

Athletes want control over their performance, and the game

plan is critical to achieving this aim. A well-devised game plan also enhances concentration and attention to quality and, furthermore, gives athletes an alternative to focusing on the score or possible outcome.

Whenever business athletes are tackling a tough task they put a game plan in place. Whether they are aiming to achieve a budget, get a new job or complete an important project, they acknowledge that it is equally as important to have a clear game plan.

Business athletes recognise that without a game plan too many things are left to chance and this potentially reduces the quality of their performance.

MIXING PERSONAL TARGETS AND GAME PLAN
Athletes in sport and business design game plans to achieve their personal targets. The following table gives two examples of how an overall objective can be converted into a personal target and then into a game plan.

	OVERALL OBJECTIVE	PERSONAL TARGET	GAME PLAN
SPORT EXAMPLE	Score below net 70 in golf	Minimum of 10 greens in regulation	Follow pre-shot ritual Choose shots carefully Maintain tempo Use active calmness
BUSINESS EXAMPLE	Gain 3 new clients this week	Minimum of 6 extra interviews	Qualify prospects Work for referrals Listen and identify need Use active calmness

> Business athletes develop a clear game plan for all
> important tasks.

PERFORMANCE RITUALS

It would be difficult, perhaps even impossible, to find a
professional athlete who does not follow a well-practised
ritual. Rituals are the fabric that holds the performance
together. Rituals allow athletes to be calmer and to use less
energy. This leads to clearer thinking, better decision making,
better focus and a better result.

The rituals employed by athletes fall into two broad
categories:

- Pre-performance rituals
- Within-performance rituals

The **within-performance** rituals vary according to the nature
of the task involved. More important at this stage, however,
are the **pre-performance rituals** because there are a number
of common elements in sporting pre-performance rituals that
are applicable to business athletes.

Pre-performance rituals for athletes can include

- diet
- sleeping patterns
- tapering of physical training
- mental preparation such as relaxation, developing game plan
  and visualisation
- travel plans
- warm-up on site

Athletes develop their rituals through experimenting until
they find the approach that works best for them.

> The purpose of a pre-performance ritual is to be
> focused mentally and physically for the commence-
> ment of competition.

How not to do it!
Business people preparing for important presentations, board meetings and other challenging situations often do a number of things which are quite contrary to this model. There are many examples of this, however five common negative examples include working very long hours in the days leading up the event; lack of physical exercise; too much food and/ or alcohol just prior to the event; no visualisation/rehearsal of the performance plan; and rushing during the final hours or minutes before the event.

Can you imagine an athlete training hard all week, having a big lunch, lacking a clear mental picture of the game plan and dashing around just prior to a world championship? No, we can't either. And yet, there are many senior executives who haven't even thought about developing a pre-performance ritual for presentations which might have multi-million-dollar consequences.

For most individuals and business teams there is usually considerable scope for improvement in the area of pre-performance rituals. The following 'Vision of the Future' shows how an effective pre-performance ritual might be developed and used.

A Vision of the Future

It is 11.00 am Tuesday and a CEO trained in business athlete approach is about to complete the final build-up for a presentation to a major account. The tactics have been discussed and decided upon and she will spend the next 40 minutes alone in her office with the door locked and all calls suspended. Her notes have been checked, her eyes are closed and within five minutes she is in a very calm state of mind. Every aspect of the presentation is visualised, including potential distractions or negatives for which a plan has been developed. Key words and affirmations are used to build self-confidence. Feelings of success from past presentations and other achievements are recalled. With the mental practice finished, she enjoys a few precious moments of rest before becoming alert again. The CEO is now ready to perform in the zone.

TASK SPLITTING

Virtually all sport and business tasks can be split into segments. Athletes call this 'splitting'. For example, lawn bowls can be split according to ends, golf into holes, swimming into laps, tennis into games and sets, baseball into innings, marathons into kilometres and so on. Similarly, annual budgets are split into quarters, conferences into sessions, meetings into agenda items, projects into tasks and so on.

Champion athletes use splitting to plan and manage their performances. The example which follows shows how an experienced 800 metre runner has developed a simple script for a performance.[13] Notice that there are no time goals set for this runner—the athlete has developed the ability to accurately judge pace, so time goals are not necessary.

Segment Plan for an 800 Metre Runner

SEGMENT	FOCUS
First 200 metres	Establish rhythm, make position
200–350 metres	Be alert for moves, relaxed shoulders
350–500 metres	Good stride length, use key words
500–600 metres	Surge slightly at 600, push for position
600–700 metres	Power! Relaxed and strong, positive
700–800 metres	Push through, drive the legs, go, go, go!

Business athletes also use splitting to manage their performance. You no doubt use splitting on many tasks, however there may be opportunities to make this more systematic. Choose an important task on which you are currently working and try the following four steps.

1. Split the task according to time, natural segments or breaks.
2. Identify at least one personal target and strategy or game plan for each segment.
3. Rehearse the plan.
4. Review the plan after completion of the task, noting how closely you followed the splits, whether the game plan worked and if the personal targets were achieved.

The following is an example of this approach.

Project: Commence planning for a major Eastside project and complete by the end of this calendar month.

SEGMENTS	ACTION PLANS FOR SEGMENTS
Define objectives	Establish specific time frames
Budgeting	Meet with finance director on Monday
Scheduling	Find or develop suitable software
Resource allocation	Source information from Divisional GMs
Monitoring information systems	Establish the planning, monitoring and control cycle
Project control	Constant comparison between plan and reality
Project termination	Evaluation and audit report

Splitting can be particularly helpful in jobs involving a degree of variety and constantly changing tasks. Under these conditions business athletes use splitting to help them shift focus from the small segments of one task to small segments of another.

Business athletes split all reasonably sized tasks into segments and have a plan for each segment. They focus on that split instead of being unnecessarily distracted by thoughts of other tasks to be done or things which are in the past.

> Business athletes split tasks into segments because this helps them to control their focus of concentration and better manage their performance.

BUSINESS ATHLETE AFFIRMATIONS
Here are some positive self-statements to create the performance attitudes you desire and to help you to begin integrating the concepts from this chapter into your daily rituals. Use them regularly.

- 'I select personal targets for each day and for the week.'
- 'I ensure that my goals are realistic because the more accurate my goal-setting the better will be my performance.'

- 'I always have a game plan and a back-up plan for important tasks.'
- 'I use rituals as the fabric that holds my performance together.'
- 'I split tasks into segments to improve my focusing and overall performance quality.'

9

PERFORMANCE IMAGINATION

> Performance quality begins with the image in your own mind.

The formalities of take-off are over. The plane levels out and the business athlete reclines his seat slightly, checking briefly over the performance plan for the afternoon's presentation. The business athlete closes his eyes, takes a few relaxing breaths and in his mind's eye imagines himself making the presentation. The images are vivid, the details intricate and the mood controlled and positive. He 'hears' the words, 'sees' the client's executive team, feels the rush of adrenalin. He is there.

After a few minutes he pauses briefly to preview the potential interference factors, for example, focusing too much on his own performance, criticism of the recent company policy on the environment and a breakdown in the audio-visual/computer link. One by one he rehearses a series of prepared positive responses and experiences the emotions that these create. He sees himself acting according to the game plan that has been decided.

He finishes by recalling the major account presentation which went so well in Los Angeles late last year and then brings himself back to the present moment. He feels refreshed, alert and ready to perform.

THE POWER OF IMAGINATION
Without imagination there would be no new ideas, no new products, no capacity to preview the future or review the past. Imagination inspires us, guides us, warns us and leads us.

Business thrives on imagination and so does sport. The difference is that athletes have been more systematic in their use of this amazing capability which we all possess. Athletes use their imagination as a performance tool; so too does the business athlete.

Imagination is not just linked to the creative occupations. Imagination can be used productively in every occupation. For example, management accountants can use their imagination to decide how to best present information; customer-service staff can devise better ways to meet and exceed the needs of a customer and engineers can use imagination to determine the best way to solve complex problems.

These are not examples of creativity in the sense of developing original ideas, but rather of the use of the imagination to visualise the best option in a set of circumstances.

This ability to use imagination to preview or visualise the future is a common characteristic of top athletes and can be a valid and highly effective performance tool in sport and in business.

THE PICTURE IN THE MIND'S EYE

Remember when we first discussed the characteristics of people performing in the zone? One of the important characteristics was that of having a **clear mental picture or image** of the movement or strategy which they are attempting. For example, a basketball player taking a free throw has a clear image of where the ball is to go and a feel for the action required. Similarly, a hockey player reads, predicts and anticipates the flow of play.

Many of our business clients, when performing in the zone, report that they can visualise or see the total picture very clearly. This helps them to read, predict and anticipate the moves of other people, markets, competitors and the economy.

World-class athletes recognise that the image or picture in their mind's eye goes a long way to determining the quality of their performance. For this reason they devote considerable time to practising the skill of visualisation so that they can make these images positive and relevant. For example, high jumpers know that their chances of success are limited unless they can conceive in their mind an image of themselves successfully clearing the bar.

Through our work with business people across a large range of occupations it has become clear that the skill of visualisation has enormous applications in business, in areas as diverse as management, sales, medicine, teaching and the arts. It is a skill business athletes develop and fine-tune to their personal needs.

> The images which you create in your mind's eye have a major impact on the nature and quality of your performance.

USING MENTAL PRACTICE

Through regular mental practice, leading athletes learn to create vivid images of performance involving all their senses. They imagine sounds, colours, textures, smells, tastes and movement to graphically capture the atmosphere and mood of the performance. As far back as 1984, over 80 per cent of Australia's Olympic team were using mental practice as part of their preparation routine. These days all Olympic athletes are aware of the processes of mental practice and most have completed a training program designed to strengthen their ability to use their mind's eye.

The same skill is used by business athletes in many different ways, including preparation for events such as presentations, meetings, telephone calls, interviews, strategic planning meetings and any potentially challenging or important situation.

As a part of their preparation for top level discussions or work on an important new project, business athletes

- visualise themselves succeeding at training and in competition
- mentally practise new or important skills and strategies
- 'see' themselves achieving their goals
- create mental images that build confidence, concentration and energy.

In sports such as diving and gymnastics, athletes even use mental practice to learn complex moves *before* physically trying them out. In much the same way, business athletes preview presentations or visualise how a new marketing brochure might appear.

WHY DOES MENTAL PRACTICE WORK?
- Mental practice is extra practice: a 'dress rehearsal' of the real thing.
- Mental practice strengthens the mind–body coordination—an athlete's brain actually fires off the same messages to the muscles as it does during the real event.
- Mental practice programs the mind by storing a positive image (like a computer program) which can be called up when needed.
- Mental practice builds self-belief at the subconscious level.

DEVELOPING 'THE MIND'S EYE'
Many athletes talk of 'the mind's eye' and considerable research has acknowledged the many benefits that performers can gain from tapping in to the power of the mind's eye.[14]

In business, with the exception of the creative occupations such as graphic arts, copywriting and advertising, there is too little emphasis on tapping the resource of the mind's eye. If you doubt this, think back through the training seminars you have attended over the years. How many have emphasised using your mind's eye, either creatively or to preview performance?

Business athletes recognise that they possess a remarkable capacity to visualise and practise mentally. This capacity can be harnessed to become an invaluable aid in the search for consistent, high quality performance.

Activity
Most people don't realise just how often they use their mind's eye in day-to-day life. The following questions illustrate some common examples of how we use our imagination. Allocate at least 15 seconds to each and see if you can find the answer in your mind's eye.
- Can you 'see' what you would really like for dinner tonight?
- What does it taste like?

- What new piece of furniture would look good in your office?
- What does the President of the United States sound like?
- Can you feel what it is like to walk along a crowded street?
- Which of your staff members is the most impressive dresser?
- How do your most comfortable shoes feel?
- What does freshly mown grass smell like?

In the activity you just completed, did you find that you are better at imagining in one or two senses and not so good at some others? This is quite common. Runners, for example, often report that they are good at imagining the *feeling* of running but not so good at actually *seeing* the scene as they run. Similarly, business athletes are often good at *seeing* a situation but not so good at experiencing the feelings that go with it.

Athletes learn to recognise their most dominant or vivid senses and use these when visualising upcoming performances. They also work at improving the less vivid areas by completing specific training activities.

During business athlete training seminars we pay a good deal of attention to developing the skill of visualising using all senses. This helps business athletes to better tap into the power of their mind's eye. With this skill, business athletes can prepare better for performance and potentially contribute more to strategic thinking activities.

PUTTING MENTAL PRACTICE INTO ACTION

Athletes use mental practice in two ways:

1. As brief snapshots of just a few seconds.
2. In a structured way, usually including a script recorded on a cassette tape.

Business athletes often make greater use of the snapshots because this approach fits better in the workplace. Nevertheless, many business athletes have scripts prepared for specific purposes, such as event preparation, stress management and developing creative ideas.

What follows is a sample of a script we have found useful as an introduction with business athletes who want to use mental practice to prepare for a presentation. This is, of course, a general script and when you develop your own script you will no doubt want to incorporate more specific aspects.

We usually ask clients to spend a few minutes calming their minds and bodies and then talk them slowly through the script.

See yourself arriving at the venue of your presentation. You have all the materials you require and feel well equipped to make a good presentation. You meet some of the people who will be at the presentation . . . You then take a few moments to set up your notes, slides and other information. You make yourself at home, adjusting things ready for your presentation. You feel a little excited and ready to focus on the key opening points of your presentation. You sit, calm yourself, briefly rehearse the first few words of the presentation. You wait to be introduced.

The introduction is completed . . . you stand, take a calming breath as you acknowledge the audience and move into position. Your opening words are clearly spoken and you feel yourself immediately settling into the presentation. You emphasise the key points and are watchful of the audience's reactions. Your voice is clear, your tempo just right. You have your plan and key points clearly in mind.

Your plan is to work through the key points and then to elaborate on each by giving clear examples. You feel calm, alert and focused. You begin to work the audience by phrasing questions that encourage them to consider issues from a personal perspective.

You notice one person who appears to be disagreeing with what you are saying and you respond by calming yourself a little and continuing to work for clarity and relevance in your message. You make a mental note that you will deal with questions later. You move off your plan briefly, getting caught up in another example which is fresh in your mind . . . You regain focus on the plan and maintain your momentum.

Later in the presentation you summarise. You are careful not to rush through the summary . . . You draw each point back to a summary slide, which participants view as you talk.

You conclude with a pre-planned final sentence that sounds very assertive and finishes the presentation on a positive, high note. You wait for questions.

The first question is a direct challenge to one of your key points and you feel yourself reacting a little against the questioner. You calm yourself, replay the slide which summarised that issue and review the points, referring to issues raised in the question and stating your position very clearly and firmly. You then go on to deal with each question in a calm and purposeful manner.

The questions have finished and you are being thanked for your presentation. As you walk from the room you give yourself an encouraging 'mental pat on the back' and later fill out your performance review sheet, noting any areas where you might improve next time.

This is a straightforward mental practice session. It takes no more than 10 minutes and leaves the business athlete feeling better prepared and therefore more confident. To experiment with the script get someone to read it to you at a slow pace. This will help you to experience the way visualisation works.

TEN STEPS TO EFFECTIVE VISUALISATION

1. USE PICTURES OR VIDEOTAPES

Athletes make their visualisations as detailed and as real as possible by watching videotapes or studying pictures of competition. Prior to the Olympics, most athletes use this technique to program their minds to associate good performance with the specific Olympic venue. If you are giving a presentation and want to develop a vivid image of the performance, then use a picture of an audience and watch a video of yourself or someone else giving a good presentation. Also, try using music that evokes the type of emotion—for example, motivation—that goes with the situation.

Organisations are starting to realise just how important it is to encourage their performers to visualise the process which leads to achievement of objectives. For example, organisations implementing total quality management programs can potentially increase the effectiveness of the program by ensuring that the messages to all staff are vivid. Accordingly, pictures, videotapes, demonstrations and diagrams are all a part of this process.

2. USE SNAPSHOTS

Most athletes prefer to do a detailed visualisation of their performance on the day before the competition. They also employ a lot of brief visualisations in the time leading up to the event. These 'snapshots' may last for no more than a few seconds. Business athletes also make considerable use of snapshots. They can use them to preview

- a completed balance sheet
- a discipline interview
- a new product
- alternative strategies
- a telephone call
- a new productivity process
- the layout of a store

Business athletes use snapshots for planning and for inspiration. There is no limit to how positive and powerful the snapshots can be. Athletes inspire themselves with their snapshots and so can you.

3. CALM BEFORE YOU CAPTURE

Before trying to capture the image you are looking for, it is best to take a few moments to calm your mind. This reduces the amount of interference and ultimately produces a better, clearer image. The business athlete recognises the value of calmness and uses it to tap into the mind's eye.

4. GO FOR THE INSIDE SHOT

Some people visualise from within their own bodies, while others do it from the outside looking in. For example, a shooter may be able to visualise from the actual position and capture all of the feelings of shooting, while another shooter can only visualise as if watching themselves perform. It is best to go for the inside image because this is more vivid and obviously gives you a real rehearsal of the situation. For example, if you are preparing for a difficult counselling session with a staff member, visualise from within your own body, seeing and hearing yourself dealing with the situation.

5. MAKE IT VIVID

Athletes strive to make their visualisation as vivid and as real as possible. They aim to engage all of their senses and include as much detail as possible. For a weightlifter this means seeing everything about the venue, including the warm-up area, location of judges, crowd, officials, timing devices and so on. Business athletes strive for vividness and look for all of the sensations, including feel (for example, writing), smell (texta pen), taste (cup of coffee), sight (the venue) and hearing (voices of the audience). This vividness increases the value they gain from visualisation.

> The more vivid the visualisation the more effective it will be in enhancing performance quality.

6. VISUALISE YOUR ATTITUDE

Before an event, athletes design strategies which include their physical plan and their mental plan. The mental plan covers

- what to concentrate or focus on (the game plan)
- any positive self-statements/thoughts
- the attitude that they are seeking

Top athletes get extra value from their mental practice when they visualise the physical and mental plan together. This means experiencing the actual thoughts and feelings that go with the performance, together with the physical experience. For example, a 100-metre sprinter will visualise a feeling of explosiveness and power at the start, together with the thoughts about form and style.

Business athletes also visualise the thoughts and attitudes that go with the performance. This can include calmness for detailed work, inspiration for creative activities, confidence for challenging tasks and so on.

7. DEAL WITH THE CHALLENGES

In sport and business things do not always go according to plan. For example, every golfer knows that there is not much point in just visualising yourself playing perfectly from tee to green. This isn't realistic. Instead, the top golfers also see themselves getting out of tough situations such as in long rough, and coping with setbacks, for example, a putt that 'lips' out.

Business athletes also recognise that an essential component of consistent, high quality performance is the ability to bounce back from setbacks, such as when a certain sale is lost. This isn't negative thinking but instead it gets them into the frame of mind needed to produce an outstanding effort under trying conditions. A good deal of the training we conduct with sales people focuses on this area.

8. SEE YOUR SUCCESSES

Nothing succeeds like success and the top Olympic and professional athletes know this and capitalise on it. They regularly recall their achievements and visualise how it looked and felt to be successful. Think back over some of your proudest achievements and then vividly recall how it felt.

9. WRAP UP THE GOOD ONES

When you put in a top performance, spend a few minutes visualising it before the images begin to fade. Ideally do it the same day. This is just like the tennis player who replays a top point in their mind to further reinforce their skills and self-belief.

10. CONDITION THE KEY WORDS

When visualising, business athletes recite words to themselves that describe how they want to feel, act or think in that situation. For example, when preparing for a particularly difficult project they might recite the word 'calm' at those times when things might be the most difficult. This is called **pre-programming** and is exactly what athletes in target sports do to create the feelings of calmness they need just before releasing the bullet or arrow. The importance of this is highlighted by reports that the former world champion archer, Rick McKinney of the United States of America, spent two hours per day visualising for his performance.

BUSINESS ATHLETE AFFIRMATIONS

Here are your affirmations to help you to begin integrating the concepts from this chapter into your daily rituals. Use them regularly.

- 'I feed my mind with positive images.'
- 'I recognise that the images I create in my mind directly influence my performance.'
- 'I use brief snapshots when preparing to perform.'

- 'I make my visualisation as vivid as possible by engaging all of my senses.'
- 'I use a mental practice script to prepare for important events.'
- 'I calm myself before visualising and this helps to make the images clearer.'
- 'I *create* the attitude that I desire by *visualising* the attitude that I desire.'
- 'I sometimes visualise myself in difficulties, then see myself meeting the challenge and succeeding.'
- 'I gain great benefit from vividly recalling my successes.'

10

BREAKING DOWN
PERFORMANCE BARRIERS

> Business athletes recognise that team work is
> essential to achieving their overall goals.

Most of us can recall an athlete who was a sure bet in a
major sporting event, but for one reason or another, performed well short of expectations. For example, who would
have bet on any of the following

- Greg Norman missing the 'cut' in the 1991 US Masters Golf.
- Mike Tyson losing his world heavyweight crown to James
  'Buster' Douglas.
- Steffi Graf failing to win a major tournament in 1990.
- the USA Men's 4 x 100 m track team being disqualified in
  the 1988 Seoul Olympics.

Sport history is full of examples of finely tuned athletes who
didn't 'put it together' on the day. In sport and in business
there are no sure bets, only firm favourites. Why? Every
performer in sport, the arts, science, business or any area
of life faces potential blocks or barriers to performing at a
consistently high level. Some of these blocks come from
within the performer—for example, thoughts, emotions—
while others originate with the outside world—for example,
other people, conditions.

Top athletes face many of these barriers and learn to
minimise the effects on performance through the use of well-
practised strategies. They know that it is impossible to
eliminate all of the barriers, but they can reduce their effects
and so be less likely to become another 'surprise loser'.

In this chapter we examine some of the barriers that inhibit peformance and show how business athletes break these down and set new limits.

TEN KEYS TO BREAKING DOWN THE BARRIERS

1. DEFEAT THE OPPONENT WITHIN

Sport is full of challenges and tests. While many of these arise out of competing against others, most top athletes say that it is the **opponent within themselves** that presents the greatest challenge.

Athletes who get on top of the inner game perform better and win more often. Similarly business athletes recognise that winning in business begins by conquering the inner game.

The inner challenges in sport and business include being able to

- confront negativity
- deal constructively with failure
- take calculated risks
- maintain patience
- harness emotions

> The successful performers in any area of life recognise that there is a battle with themselves to win before they win the battle with their opponents.

2. REMEMBER EPICTETUS

More than 2000 years ago the Greek philosopher Epictetus said, 'We are not disturbed by things but rather by the view that we take of them.'

Had Epictetus been a sporting fan he might have cited the following example to illustrate his point.

Two golfers of equal ability, Richard and Geoff, are playing together and are level with the card as they reach the seventeenth tee. The seventeenth is a long par three with a small, circular lake on the right near the front edge of the gently sloping green. Geoff plays first using a three iron, but fades the ball a little too much and it splashes into the lake. Richard, seeing this happen, selects a three wood and steps up to the tee. He strikes the ball well but a little too high. The breeze, which is blowing from left to right, catches the ball as it slows, causing it to land in the left-hand corner of the lake.

As the players walk towards the lake, Geoff is relaxed and readying himself for the next shot. It will require a short shot with a pitching wedge from the position where he will drop a new ball, near the edge of the lake. Richard, on the other hand, is quite upset. He is thinking about the damage that he has done to his score and is cursing his bad luck.

Geoff and Richard have interpreted virtually the same event in quite different ways. This is summarised in the following table.

Geoff

THE EVENT	THE REACTION	THE 'VIEW'
Hit the ball into the lake on the seventeenth hole.	Disappointment and then into a problem-solving approach. Focuses on making the best possible next shot.	'It would have been better if I hadn't hit the ball in the lake, however that's done so I'll make the next shot great.'

Richard

THE EVENT	THE REACTION	THE 'VIEW'
Hit the ball into the lake on the seventeenth hole.	Frustrated, angry with himself and then despondent. Not task-focused for the next shot.	'I *shouldn't* have hit the ball in the lake. I've ruined the round. I *always* get the bad luck.'

Examples of business situations equivalent to hitting the ball into the lake include

- a top staff member resigns
- the computer hard disk crashes
- a supplier reneges on a commitment
- being retrenched
- a change in economic conditions

In business and in sport it is important to recognise that it is not the event that causes us to be upset but rather the view we take of the event. Business athletes use this knowledge to develop greater control over their inner game.

Business athletes choose how to react to situations.

---

3. AVOID PERFECTIONIST THINKING

Business athletes learn from examples like the previous golfing anecdote, because so many performance barriers are triggered by the type of perfectionist thinking shown by Richard. The irony is that Richard desperately wants to do well but it is Geoff who has been able to translate a desire to do well into a calm, 'get on with the job' attitude.

Too often in business the desire to win the sale or to make the perfect presentation ends up being so all-consuming that it actually reduces performance significantly.

Emotional upsets are often caused by seeing situations in terms of 'should', 'must' or 'have to'. Common examples include:

- 'People should be more efficient.'
- 'I have to go to that meeting.'
- 'You must do the right thing and tell the boss.'
- 'Computers shouldn't break down.'
- 'He can't resign.'
- 'Suppliers must meet their commitments.'

The following example shows the link between an event, the reaction to the event and the attitude taken.

THE EVENT	THE REACTION	THE 'ATTITUDE'
A customer suggests that a main product is inferior to a competitor's line.	Annoyed, angry.	'People shouldn't criticise something that they don't know anything about.' 'The man's a fool.'

When reviewing situations where they have lost control of their performance during competition, top athletes often

report that it was caused by putting unnecessary pressure on themselves. This usually means thinking in a way which is negative, unrealistic and/or 'perfectionist'.
Can you recall a time when this happened to you?

4. USE PERFORMANCE THINKING
Business athletes convert perfectionist thoughts or statements into performance statements. In this way they avoid becoming distracted from their main priorities.

Perfectionist thinking is contrasted with performance thinking in the following table. Examples for sport and business are outlined.

Perfectionist thinking	Performance thinking
SPORT	SPORT
'I shouldn't have dropped the ball.'	'I dropped the ball.'
'The umpire should have seen it.'	'The umpire made a mistake, now get on with my job.'
BUSINESS	BUSINESS
'The Board should have been more open to my ideas.'	'There are ways to get this project through and I'll find them.'
'I must get a sale.'	'I am going to make 10 extra calls and present at my best each time.'
'Jenny should have written down the message.'	'I wish Jenny had written down the message however she didn't, so I'd better get on and re-build with the client.'
'My manager should be more positive.'	'It would be better if my manager was more positive however I'll focus on doing my job as well as I can.'
'I mustn't make a mistake.'	'Let's go for it and do it with style.'
'We should have won the tender.'	'We could have won and we didn't, but we learnt something for next time.'

What differences do you notice between perfectionist and performance thinking?

5. SEPARATE THE MOTIVATION FROM THE PRESSURE

Business athletes distinguish between challenge and pressure. They also recognise that something which is challenging in certain conditions can create unnecessary pressure under different circumstances.

For example, in a positive environment, the statement, 'We have to beat budget', can really challenge and motivate the 'troops'. In a recession or after a setback, however, it can lead to needless pressure. Under these circumstances, it can be better to focus on short-term performance statements and goals, such as, 'Let's each get in front of five extra customers'. This is a challenge and focuses attention on the task.

6. TEAM COMMUNICATION

Good basketball teams invariably place a lot of emphasis on good communication on and off the court. They find that it is easier for individuals to handle the difficult times if there is support and encouragement from other team members.

In our work with professional sporting teams we always encourage the whole team to set specific goals for communication. This includes specifying what actually constitutes high quality communication.

Interestingly, most athletes when asked to review team performance report that the first thing to break down under pressure is communication. The same is often true of business organisations.

Business athletes maintain high quality communication within and outside their immediate team. They know that they can best achieve their goals through an effective and well-performing team.

One of the most effective ways of getting past the performance barrier is through a concerted team effort. Communication is one of the foundations on which that effort is constructed.

7. BE AWARE OF THE 'BANNISTER EFFECT'

The **Bannister effect** is the phenomenon where athletes reach a plateau or barrier which seems to be impossible to surpass.

The term the 'Bannister effect' originated with Roger Bannister, the first person to break the four-minute-mile barrier. The four-minute barrier halted the previously steady lowering of record times for a number of years. As soon as Bannister broke through the barrier, other runners also bettered the four-minute mark and the steady reduction in times continued again.

The Bannister effect occurs in business and in many other areas of life. For example, it might be argued that the continued reliance on the internal combustion engine is actually an example of a Bannister effect. Certainly, there are many instances in business where people stop progressing because of a real or imagined barrier. Some common examples include being 'stuck' at a career level such as middle management, being unable to gain extra market share, being unable to move into new markets, being unable to change career direction.

There are three key steps in eliminating a Bannister effect.

1. Recognise that it exists.
2. Determine a process that will push through it.
3. Commit to that process.

In the case of the four-minute mile there was considerable scientific and populist evidence put forward to prove that it was physically impossible to run a sub-four-minute mile. Similarly, it is not unusual to be told in business that something is impossible. When this occurs the business athlete recognises that many people consider impossible as meaning 'too hard'. Just as Bannister committed himself to the process of training at a new level, so too do business athletes increase the quality at each stage of the process that leads to breaking through their barriers. This has the dual effect of improving performance and distracting focus away from the barrier.

Can you think of a Bannister effect that occurs in your profession?

When faced with a Bannister effect, business athletes focus on increasing quality at each stage of the process.

8. SEEK SUCCESS

A league soccer team was leading the competition with eight matches to the end of the season. The coach decided that the best strategy for the remainder of the season would be to go defensive to avoid losing. Needless to say, the team performed badly and after a loss and two draws with poorer teams, was soon in a position where they might lose the championship. A performance psychologist was called in when there were four games remaining, and after a team meeting it was agreed that the team's best game plan was to attack. For the remainder of the season they decided to play like the best attacking team in the competition. They quickly regained their winning ways and while they had quite a few goals scored against them, they simply out-ran the opposition. They subsequently won the championship.

Under competitive conditions, athletes often take calculated risks in search of success. These athletes seek success and look forward to challenges. They are not afraid of failure and try to take control of the situation. The most consistently successful performers are those who take calculated risks in seeking out success. The old adage 'fortune favours the brave' reflects the feeling held by many sport lovers that sport rewards those performers who are prepared to be positive.

Business athletes face many situations where there is a choice between seeking success or taking a more conservative approach. Generally the business athlete seeks out success.

This doesn't mean being foolhardy. Top performers 'play the percentages' and make full use of their own skills. They do this by focusing on what they *do* want to happen, rather than paying heed to what they *don't* want to happen. The two examples that follow illustrate this point.

Emily, an account executive for an international advertising and media relations firm, found that her performance had slumped from previously high levels. On analysing her performance-management style, it became clear that Emily had gradually become less bold in her search for new clients, preferring to work mainly in areas where she felt comfortable. Having recognised this, Emily rectified the situation by gradually expanding her prospecting activities. Within three months, she had regained her previous performance levels and her confidence had returned.

The Chief Executive Officer of a large organisation was very concerned that staff not make errors. His management team gradually became less and less inclined to take decisions without first checking on his attitude to the issue. This resulted in reduced morale, deteriorating customer service and an increase in staff turnover. The CEO was made aware of the effect that this style of management was having on the organisation. He took steps to ensure that staff were rewarded for responding quickly to matters which fell generally under company policy.

A success-oriented business athlete

- is results-oriented
- looks for new opportunities
- sets challenging targets
- isn't concerned by negative people
- weighs up the options and then acts
- communicates the vision clearly
- views setbacks as opportunities

> When faced with a choice between avoiding failure and approaching success, business athletes look first towards success and, if they can afford the costs, they go for it.

9. LEARN TO MANAGE DEFEAT

There is a quiz question which asks contestants to nominate how many tennis matches need to be played if there are 128 players in the tournament. While most people think that there is a difficult formula required, the answer is 127. Simply, every player loses once, except for the eventual winner.

The point is, of course, that losing is an integral part of sport, and while few top performers like it they are skilled at dealing with loss. There are two strategies most commonly used by athletes following a defeat.

1. Using the defeat as a *learning experience* and as *motivation* to train even harder and prepare more thoroughly
2. Focusing on the *quality* of the performance and so deflecting thoughts away from the outcome

The pain of defeat sometimes makes it difficult to get on with either of these two steps; however, good athletes move quickly from the emotion to a more rational analysis of what happened. Within that analysis the athletes don't make excuses but instead look to use the experience as a source of information and motivation.

Business athletes also consider the quality of their performance and aim to learn something from every experience whether it be positive or negative. Many people, in fact, point to their worst experiences as being among their best learning opportunities.

Examples of things learnt from business defeats include:

- prepare better
- don't rely on other people
- always have a back-up plan
- be calm and let things flow
- always put in your best possible proposal
- keep company details confidential
- engage others' help early in the project

What have been some of your defeats and what did you learn from them?

> There is no such thing as a defeat if something is gained which will help you to be better next time.

10. BE A REALISTIC OPTIMIST

Most athletes, at some stage in their careers, go through periods when their thinking becomes negative. During these stages top athletes make an effort to create a more positive and optimistic outlook. They achieve this by systematically tackling each negative thought and replacing it with a more optimistic alternative. To do this effectively involves five simple steps and a degree of diligence. Follow these steps when you want to develop a more positive and optimistic outlook.

1. Record the thoughts that create emotion

Over a period of one week make a list of those thoughts that seem to trigger either a positive or negative change of mood. For example, thoughts about a work colleague might cause you to feel less motivated, while thoughts about your family might make you feel very optimistic and on top of things.

Optimistic thoughts reported by business athletes include

- 'I'm relaxed and ready to go.'
- 'I feel healthy and energetic.'
- 'My staff are well qualified and effective.'
- 'This company is really going somewhere.'
- 'I'm going to win this account.'
- 'Let's increase market share during the recession.'

2. Review each negative thought

At the end of the week, go over all of the negative thoughts. In particular, look for those times when you have exaggerated, been overly pessimistic or just negative.

Negative thoughts reported by business athletes include

- 'It looks like an opportunity is never going to arise.'
- 'I'll never get through all this paperwork.'
- 'I'll never understand this computer system.'
- 'No one can make money in this recession.'
- 'I wish I'd done that course.'
- 'The board will probably reject the plan.'
- 'Someone will always get the promotion ahead of me.'

3. Develop alternatives

Review the negative thoughts you have recorded and, one by one, develop a more optimistic alternative. For example, instead of thinking 'I hope I don't make a mistake' an alternative can be, 'I hope I get a chance to have a go'.

Athletes also use statements about past successes, or about their strengths, such as 'I've done well before at this level of competition'. This reference to past success builds confidence and creates a more optimistic outlook.

Business athletes have a history of success and they use

the memory of these successes to build confidence. For example, a business athlete with a particularly difficult meeting to chair might recall a similar meeting which was successful.

Some examples of more optimistic alternatives follow.

NEGATIVE SELF-TALK	REPLACEMENT ATTITUDE
'No one can make money in this recession.'	'We can build our market share and be ready for the up-turn.'
'I'm worried that it won't work out.'	'I'm going to focus on doing the basic things really well and let the result take care of itself.'
'I wish I'd done that course.'	'It's never too late to learn, so I'll do another course.'
I'll never get through all this paperwork.'	'Let's divide it into priorities and tackle them one at a time.'

4. Say no to pessimism

Even world champions experience brief moments of self-doubt. It is human nature to consider both positive and negative consequences, however these champions strive to conquer the negatives. One of the simplest ways they do this is by simply saying no, whenever they become aware of a pessimistic thought.

Ultra marathon runners use this technique when they detect a negative thought process beginning, for example, 'I'm tired, I think I'll stop'. They stop the pessimistic thought and replace it with a practical, optimistic thought, such as 'OK, let's achieve the next goal'.

Business athletes use thought-stopping immediately that they become aware of the pessimistic thought entering their minds and then replace it with a prepared alternative.

> Business athletes say no whenever they notice a pessimistic thought and replace it with an appropriate optimistic thought.

5. *Use performance words*

Many athletes use words or phrases such as 'power', 'smooth', 'with style' and 'explode' to help generate the types of feelings and intensity that they require.

Business athletes also use key words to create the state of mind appropriate to dealing with various performance situations. Examples of words used by business athletes include

- calm
- successful
- self-assured
- tidy
- focused

BUSINESS ATHLETE AFFIRMATIONS

The following self-statements or affirmations will help you to begin integrating the concepts from this chapter into your daily rituals. Use them regularly.

- 'I recognise my self-imposed performance barriers and every day become better at dealing with them.'
- 'I have an optimistic, "go for it" attitude.'
- 'I minimise my use of the words "should", "must" and "have to".'
- 'I see defeat as one of the best learning opportunities and make the most of these situations.'
- 'I have an optimistic, task-oriented approach to even the toughest situations.'

11

EVENT PREPARATION AND REVIEW

> Business athletes are better prepared than their competitors.

Top international athletes, particularly those in Olympic sports, train for months or even years for just one event. For example, the Australian Cycling team taper off their very intensive training program only for world championships and the Olympic Games. This means that all their emphasis is on preparing to perform on a specific day or consecutive days. What a contrast to most weekend athletes who compete week after week knowing that if things don't work today there is always another chance next week.

Many of the skills described in this book are used by athletes to prepare for big events. In this chapter we look at how business athletes use these same skills to prepare for important events. Some of the important events nominated by clients who have completed business athlete training include:

- a major marketing presentation (advertising agency director)
- international travel to visit key potential clients (chief executive officer)
- organising and convening a conference (sales manager)
- preparing the company budget (financial controller)
- handling a difficult discipline interview (departmental manager)
- dealing with a particularly hectic work period (secretary)
- implementing a total quality management program (first-line supervisor)

116

Each of these events requires specific personal or job-related skills. In each case, business athletes recognise that they have the necessary technical skills but need to be mentally tuned in to really put together a top performance.

WHY PREPARE FOR AN EVENT?

One of the distinguishing factors between elite athletes and those who perform at a lower level is the quality of their preparation. Elite athletes are simply better prepared. They allocate specific time to mentally prepare for competition and this enhances their performance in the competition itself.

Business athletes take the lead from their sporting counterparts by ensuring that they are better prepared than their competitors. This means being better prepared technically with information and skills as well as being better prepared physically and mentally.

While every activity, whether in sport or business, has its own special characteristics, there are some guidelines for physical and mental preparation.

1. GET READY PHYSICALLY

For athletes, the final physical preparation for an event usually begins at the time of the pre-event taper. At this point the amount of training is gradually reduced with the aim of having the athlete in the best possible physical shape on the day of competition. The pre-event taper has received considerable scientific attention, particularly in sports like athletics and swimming where performance is so much dependent on the athlete's energy. In sports such as tennis, basketball and squash the tapering process is made more difficult because the tournament may extend over a period of two weeks or more, as with Grand Slam tennis tournaments.

In the final days before competition and during the competition period, leading athletes carefully control their diet, sleeping patterns and other routines that might affect their physical state. In events extending over a long period with breaks in between, for example, the decathlon, athletes have a plan for eating, conserving energy and re-psyching before the next event.

On the day of competition athletes go through a specific, well-rehearsed warm-up strategy designed to ready their body for peak performance. The intensity of this warm-up will vary according to the psych-up level appropriate for that event: weightlifters get very psyched while archers stretch, loosen and remain very calm.

Business athletes also recognise that their ability to perform at a high level, particularly over an extended period, is partly dependent on their energy level. They exercise regularly, follow a low-fat diet, keep alcohol consumption to a controlled minimum, and monitor their energy levels. A business person who doesn't maintain an adequate energy level simply cannot perform at their best. Signs of this include

- drowsiness during the day
- lack of energy
- no creativity or 'spark'
- increased errors
- poor handling of an interpersonal situation

Each of these signs reflects a breakdown in the application of skills in much the same way as a tennis player's ability to play shots diminishes as tiredness takes over. Perhaps the tennis player's breakdown is more obvious, but the damage done by tired executives could possibly be measured in millions of dollars.

Business athletes monitor their performance and, like the athlete, develop a pre-performance ritual that gets them into the best possible physical condition. Similarly, during pro-longed periods of high intensity work they use many of the strategies employed by the decathlete. Some of these more common strategies include

- maintaining a regular sleeping pattern if at all possible
- using any 'down-time' between activities for rest and recovery
- eating light foods that are easily digested
- taking every opportunity to get some fresh air
- taking short breaks
- maintaining good physical condition

> Business athletes use the down-time between activities to be in the best possible physical and mental state for important events.

2. GET READY MENTALLY

For most leading athletes their mental preparation includes planning of strategies for competition—the game plan—and development of an emotional state or mood. While these are closely related, it is important to realise that doing one well does not guarantee the other. For example, an athlete may be perfectly psyched up for an event, only to be caught out because they don't have a game plan to combat their opponents' strengths. Similarly, an athlete with a great game plan is going nowhere if they are not sufficiently psyched up to put it into action.

Develop the game plan

The development of strategies for an important event requires a study of the conditions and, if appropriate, the opposition. We have already emphasised that one of the keys to the success of international athletes is that they are better prepared than their opponents. Central to this preparation is scouting—that is, having information about themselves, the conditions and their opponents.

Consider the example of an Olympic hockey team. Their preparation includes keeping detailed statistics on their own performances together with finding out about such things as

- travel arrangements
- living conditions (meals, room arrangements)
- nature of the venue
- likely weather and pitch conditions
- timing of matches
- any special rules
- specific strengths of opposition
- likely opposition match strategies

Top performers make sure that they control all of those things which can be controlled. Having information moves them one step closer to establishing that control.

Business athletes preparing for a presentation also set out to gather information and establish control. A check list of controllables might include many of the following:

- agreed on specific topics
- know audience characteristics

- overhead projector with spare globe
- pens, whiteboard and chart paper
- position of podium checked
- slides prepared and checked
- full rehearsal completed
- throat lozenges and a glass of water on podium

Use rituals to find the zone
Athletes know that the key to getting into the right emotional state is to develop rituals that are completed prior to and during each performance. These rituals increase certainty, enhance confidence and lead to better performance. Getting ready emotionally also means developing the emotional state or intensity which accompanies or triggers your best performances. This means reducing the negative influences of fatigue, frustration, anxiety and anger while building confidence and energy.

As we have seen, techniques such as calming, self-hypnosis, performance meditation and visualisation are used by athletes in sport and business to develop this ideal emotional state.

In the business athlete training conducted in industry, participants work individually to develop strategies for achieving the ideal emotional state prior to an event. In each case, these people learn to recognise their zone and develop rituals designed to get them into their zone when required.

PUTTING TOGETHER A PRE-EVENT RITUAL

LOOK IN YOUR OWN 'BACKYARD'
The most effective method for developing your own pre-event ritual is to recall and review your own experiences in past events. These events are full of information about activities which helped or hindered your performance. The following questions will help to initiate the review; however, don't be limited just to these questions.

Do I usually get mentally ready for an important event?	yes/no	(why?)
Am I usually focused at the start of such an event?	yes/no	(why?)
Do I have a ritual for preparing for important events?	yes/no	(why?)

Can my ritual be used in most key events?   yes/no   (why?)

Do circumstances tend to upset my routine?   yes/no   (why?)

When consulting with athletes or teams, we regularly encourage them to complete an activity called 'performance contrasting'. In this activity, the athletes or teams choose up to six past performances and rate their performance quality on a scale from 1 (poor) to 7 (excellent). The poorer and the better performances are then analysed and contrasted, using a detailed checklist, to establish the triggers for various levels of performance. A similar format has been used with considerable success in the sales field.

> Business athletes analyse their own performances and extract useful information to help them identify their performance triggers.

DEVELOP TEAM RITUALS

Successful teams almost always have consistent rituals and these become the standards that new members are expected to uphold. The rituals have been developed over some time and players recognise that their success is dependent upon every player maintaining these standards.

Successful business athlete teams recognise that they benefit from having good team players who follow the rituals and standards established over years of performance.

SCOUT THE OPPOSITION

Top football and basketball coaches report that a significant contributor to their team performance is the knowledge they have about their opposition. This knowledge helps them to plan and practise strategies which will either counteract their opponents' strengths or exploit weaknesses.

Many teams use check lists when viewing opposition games to ensure that they capture all of the important information. In football, a check list might include offensive patterns, reactions to opposition scoring, potential flexibility of players to shift position, defensive patterns, timing of plays and so on.

Business athletes are also interested in collecting information about opposition products, possible changes in government policy, sources of finance and other aspects relevant to their position.

ADJUST TO DIFFERENT LOCATIONS

The location of an event will often markedly influence your preparation. Some athletes find the absence of facilities such as warm-up areas to be a distraction, however the top performers always have an alternative warm-up that can be done anywhere at any time.

Business athletes often perform outside their own office environment and therefore it is vital that they are able to adapt their pre-event rituals to suit the conditions in which they find themselves.

When developing your pre-event rituals consider the type of environment in which you will be performing and structure the ritual accordingly.

DON'T SABOTAGE YOUR OWN EFFORTS

We often see athletes who have sabotaged their own efforts by forgetting their rituals and doing things differently when they go to important competitions. This often comes from wanting to do very well and can include following an unfamiliar warm-up ritual, or thinking too much about the event.

> Business athletes develop rituals for important events.

A check list used by athletes to develop a pre-competition ritual is outlined below to give you further ideas for aspects which you might build into your own rituals.

_____ travel arrangements
_____ event times
_____ check-in times
_____ meal times
_____ diet plan
_____ timing of equipment check
_____ content of competition plan/strategy

_____ content of back-up plan
_____ meet with coach
_____ timing of mental practice
_____ warm-up ritual
_____ warm-up time
_____ likely weather conditions
_____ post-event warm-down
_____ post-competition review

PERFORMANCE REVIEW

Performance review is one of the most neglected areas in sport and business and yet it provides such a rich opportunity to learn about your performance and to improve for next time.

In sport, a post-performance review involves a complete debriefing, usually by the athletes in conjunction with the coach. The process followed by many athletes is to design a post-event review format which provides for ratings in the key areas of

- quality of preparation
- quality of skills
- quality of mental approach
- quality of physical performance

Each area is divided into a number of sub-areas, for example, the physical area may be divided into speed, agility, endurance, reaction, strength and power. Athletes then rate their performance in each area on a 1–7 scale ranging from poor to excellent.

This type of review provides a more thorough appraisal of performance than the shallow attempts that tend to look at performance as either good or bad. Top athletes recognise that a thorough performance review provides invaluable input into their future training and competition strategies.

In business, the traditional appraisal of performance is usually done by someone else and anything up to 12 months after the event. The business athlete rejects this type of system as being too judgmental and not geared to a rapid change in performance.

Business athletes regularly complete brief self-appraisals and seek the feedback of others to verify or add to the appraisal. In this way feedback is more immediate and relevant to their performance.

> Business athletes regularly complete brief self-appraisals and seek the feedback of others to verify or add to the appraisal.

BUSINESS ATHLETE AFFIRMATIONS

Below are some positive self-statements to help you to begin integrating the concepts from this chapter into your daily rituals. Use them regularly.

- 'I am better prepared than my competitors.'
- 'I prepare physically, mentally and emotionally for important events.'
- 'I maintain an adequate energy level.'
- 'I control the controllables.'
- 'I have rituals for prior to and during each performance.'
- 'My team has consistent rituals that they follow and these are the standards which new members are expected to uphold.'
- 'I review each performance and this information helps me to do better in the future.'
- 'I regularly complete brief self-appraisals and seek feedback from others to add to the quality of my performance.'

12

FIT BODY, FIT MIND

> Business athletes recognise the contribution that
> health and fitness make towards maintaining
> consistent, high quality performance.

The Olympic motto, *'Citius, altius, fortius'* (Faster, higher, stronger), reflects the physical qualities of the Olympic athlete. While the winner of the Olympic decathlon is the epitome of a physical athlete, every event from archery to the marathon demands physical and mental excellence.

Only recently have physical fitness and health been acknowledged as important in determining the performance of people in other than physical occupations such as fire-fighting and labouring. Organisations have begun to experiment with health and fitness programs for their staff and have found that a healthier and fitter workforce means a healthier bottom line for the organisation. The key question is, of course, what constitutes health and fitness for a business athlete?

Business athletes define physical fitness or health according to their specific needs or desires. For example, they might need or want to develop fitness for work, recreation, family activities or social reasons. Interestingly, many business people gain their fitness for work from the need to be fit to meet the demands in some other area of their life—for example, to maintain a hobby farm, to compete in fun runs, to stay attractive to the opposite sex.

Typical white-collar workers can usually complete their work tasks on a given day with a relatively poor level of fitness compared with that needed for even moderately demanding activities such as playing tennis, walking briskly up a hill or shovelling a few loads of sand. In contrast, athletes such as squash players, basketballers and tennis players ensure that they are physically tuned to perform consistently over a long period of time, for example throughout a tournament or even a season.

Business athletes take the lead from sportspeople by viewing physical fitness from a more professional perspective than just having the ability to do one activity on one day. Business is an endurance event and business athletes see numerous potential benefits in maintaining an adequate level of physical fitness. These can include

- more energy to devote to each work task
- more energy for family activities
- clearer thinking due to less tension
- better overall quality of life
- more endurance to cope with demanding work periods
- fewer aches and pains such as headaches and back pain

Can you benefit by improving your physical fitness?

The steps taken by the business athlete to develop and maintain an appropriate level of physical health and fitness are explained in the following sections.

ESTABLISH A BENCHMARK

Most athletes begin their pre-season training with an assessment of their current fitness level. In Olympic endurance sports this involves a detailed series of measurements carried out in a laboratory by an exercise physiologist and includes tests for percentage of body fat, blood lactate, oxygen consumption and flexibility. Various field tests such as a timed five-minute run and a standing jump test can also be included.

Business athletes establish a benchmark for fitness prior to commencing training or moving into a more intensive phase. The type of testing undertaken by business athletes replicates many of the tests taken by athletes, although they do not involve maximum exertion. For instance, a bicycle test is conducted at sub-maximal exertion.

The testing is undertaken to determine any underlying medical conditions which need treatment, such as raised blood pressure; any physical conditions which need to be taken into account when developing the activity program, for example, restricted joint mobility; and the best possible activity program for the particular business athlete. The information gathered from the assessment is used to establish a baseline against which improvements can be measured. Business athletes use this baseline as a benchmark to set goals and monitor improvement in many different areas. For instance, there may be a need to reduce weight, improve flexibility, or establish better tolerance to exercise.

There is a real danger in undertaking a training program without first ensuring that it will not be potentially dangerous. If you see scope and benefits in improving your fitness, then complete a thorough medical assessment and, with the approval of your physician, begin slowly under the supervision of a qualified instructor.

> Business athletes do not have to be fit enough to run marathons. Rather, business athletes recognise that their long-term quality of work and life is related to their physical health and fitness.

GO FOR ACTIVITY, NOT INTENSITY

Alex is a partner in a medium-sized national legal practice. She attended a conference on the theme of 'Better Fitness, Better Performance' and, following the conference, decided to put the concept into practice and join a local health club. Alex did two sessions of aerobics and two sessions of a super-circuit—a timed circuit of weights—each week.

During the first month, Alex improved quickly, had more energy at work and felt much better about herself.

In the second month, Alex started to set progressively more difficult goals for herself. This meant doing an hour of the most advanced aerobics class and increasing weights and repetitions during the super circuit. Soon she was feeling tired at work and was struggling to meet her training goals.

By the third month Alex was skipping training sessions and by mid-way through the next month had sustained an injury to her back. A week later she decided to give up exercising.

Have you ever been through an experience like Alex's?

Alex forgot her original goal and let her natural achievement motivation take over. Soon her training went from active and rejuvenating to very intense and exhausting.

Athletes and coaches sometimes fall into the trap of believing that if a bit of activity is good for you, then twice as much must be twice as good.

For business athletes the key to fitness training is viewing activity as the goal, rather than wanting to reach Olympic levels of fitness. This means asking two key questions. Firstly, what is my goal? And secondly, how is this helping me to achieve my goal?

It is to be hoped that if Alex can be enticed back into a physical activity program she will ask these questions before again letting the 'achievement bug' take control.

In the next few years we are likely to see a trend away from intense and potentially damaging forms of exercise. Instead, emphasis will be on regular, daily activity which will be as much a part of the routine as cleaning the teeth.

For business athletes the key to fitness training is to view activity as the goal.

FIND A PROGRAM THAT SUITS

Any top coach will tell you that the ideal physical program is one that prepares athletes physically while keeping them interested and motivated. For this reason, most Olympic and professional sports follow fitness programs which include a wide variety of training methods, including

- free weights
- machine weights
- distance running
- sprinting
- sandhill training
- swimming
- cross-sport activities (for example, volleyballers playing basketball)

Business athletes also take into account their goals for fitness and their own preference for activities. A few years ago the options for training seemed to be limited to running and weight training but now the options are much more varied. If you are constructing your own program some of the options available include

- power walking
- low-impact aerobics
- swimming or aqua-aerobics
- super circuit
- jogging on soft surfaces
- weight training
- sports such as golf, tennis

To design a program which suits you, begin by collecting information on the range of activities that are available. Visit health and fitness centres, talk with friends or colleagues and chat with your fitness adviser during your initial assessment. There are a number of options available to you in arranging your training.

Training alone
The main advantage of training alone is the freedom it allows you. If you can maintain the discipline and enjoy having time to yourself, then this might be a good option.

Training with a partner
Many business athletes have a training partner. This helps them to keep going at times when they might lose a bit of willpower and perhaps go for a drink at the local club instead. Make sure that your training partner has similar goals, otherwise the relationship probably won't last too long.

Find a suitable time
The time that you train might be determined by your work schedule or by your own preference. Some people find that it is best to train early in the morning before work, while for others this is a nightmare they couldn't keep up for more than a few days. Consider your schedule and preferences before deciding on the timing of your training sessions.

Varied program or settled?
If you tend to get bored easily and need a lot of variety then perhaps a program with a number of different activities

might help. This could mean changing activities each day or doing block training—for example, a week of swimming then a week of jogging and so on. Before you begin block training discuss the program with your fitness adviser to make sure that you are not getting too much or too little of one type of training. For example, if you do only aerobic exercise for a few weeks—running, power walking, aerobics— the muscle tone in your upper body may deteriorate. In this case your instructor might suggest building a week of super circuit or swimming into your program.

Rigid routine or less structured?
Some people like to follow a very rigid, well-structured program and others prefer a more instinctive style. For example, one runner might structure a session for a certain time or distance while another might just run as fast, and for as long, as feels comfortable.

GET LOOSE, STAY LOOSE
One of the most important activities in an athlete's pre- and post-training and competition routine is the stretching of the muscles. This is done to prevent injury, increase overall flexibility and ultimately to add to performance.

There are also many benefits for business athletes in stretching not only prior to exercise but also at other times during the day. These include freedom of movement, less pain from sore joints and less risk of injury during exercise.

Loss of flexibility accompanies ageing, and if you are in a sedentary occupation there is an increased risk that your range of movement will decline significantly with age. Also, if you experience arthritis, then maintaining flexibility through activity is essential in managing the condition.

Business athletes generally report that they perform better when they are active and supple. They also recover more quickly from long periods of confined travel such as international flights.

Stretching is done in two ways. In **static stretching** you extend each muscle from a point of rest to extension. Touching the toes is an example of static stretching; the hamstring and back muscles are extended.

Dynamic stretching takes you through a more active

routine. In sport this often simulates the actual moves made during training or competition. Baseball pitchers moving their arms in a throwing motion is a form of dynamic stretching.

When you begin your activity program make a point of stretching before and after the activity. Seek advice from your instructor about the best approach for your needs.

WILL YOU BECOME WHAT YOU EAT?
The relationship between diet and performance is well known. Athletes plan their intake of food and liquid to ensure that they have sufficient energy to meet the demands of training and competition.

The diet chosen by an athlete reflects the type of training with which they are involved. For example, an athlete doing heavy weight training is likely to be on a diet high in protein, while an athlete getting ready to compete in a marathon the next day will consume a meal high in carbohydrate to provide energy for the body to burn during the event.

It is not the purpose of this book to provide a detailed coverage of nutrition, although during business athlete training programs we use a nutritionist to consult with participants. Business athletes recognise that different foods have different effects on their metabolism. Generally, they avoid foods with high fat content, such as fried foods and pies, and instead seek a balanced diet. They avoid the traditional business lunch, rarely consume more than one glass of alcohol at lunch and restrict their overall alcohol consumption.

NO DRUGS
The 1990s have seen the demise of the drug cheat in sport, although in the wider community there has been an increase in the use of drugs.

The most common drugs used by business people are alcohol, caffeine and tobacco, although prescription drugs and so-called recreational drugs such as cocaine and marijuana are becoming increasingly common.

The sporting community has been insistent that performance-enhancing drugs have no place in sport, and the testing procedures now in place make it difficult for any athlete to take drugs and avoid detection.

Business athletes recognise that the use of drugs to enhance performance, such as alcohol to control anxiety, leads to even less control, even if short-term performance gains appear. Instead the business athlete learns to control or manage tension and other emotions through some of the techniques covered in this book.

If at some time you contemplate using drugs to help you in any area of your life, make absolutely sure that your dosage is being controlled by a responsible physician. Do not take the drugs for one day more than is necessary and get a second opinion if you feel that the drugs are starting to take control of your life.

BUSINESS ATHLETE AFFIRMATIONS

The affirmations listed below will help you begin integrating the concepts from this chapter into your daily rituals. Use them regularly.

- 'I establish a benchmark for health and fitness prior to commencing training or moving into a more intensive training phase.'
- 'Activity is the goal of my fitness program.'
- 'I enjoy being active and healthy.'
- 'I stretch prior to exercise and at other times during the day.'
- 'I cat healthy foods.'

13

THE BUSINESS COACH

> Business coaches are leaders, teachers, role models and counsellors.

Many business athletes lead teams or whole organisations and their success is dependent upon their ability to produce good quality performance from their staff on a consistent basis.

Coaching is a loosely defined activity which can describe anything from the teaching of simple skills to the hellfire and brimstone speech for which some sporting coaches have become famous. Dr Rainer Martens, an internationally renowned sport psychologist, describes the role of coaches as '. . . helping athletes to develop their physical, psychological and social abilities to their greatest potential'.[15]

Sport coaches employ the science and art of coaching to assist athletes to produce consistent, high quality performance. Many of the principles of sport coaching have direct relevance and benefit for business athletes.

In this chapter we introduce the concept of the business coach and discuss some key areas you may wish to explore further if your role involves coaching.

THE FOUR MAIN ROLES OF THE BUSINESS COACH
While coaches in sport and business fill many roles, there are four key roles that directly influence team performance.

1. Leader
2. Teacher
3. Model
4. Counsellor

1. LEADER

All leaders in sport and business have a leadership style which characterises the way they go about managing or coaching. Some coaches are predominantly autocratic or authoritarian. They issue very firm, unequivocal instructions, make most decisions themselves and are highly task-oriented. Other coaches are very democratic in style and are concerned with developing good relationships and a positive team culture. In between these styles are those coaches who balance the need for good relationships and team culture with the recognition that there is a task to be done.

Experience and common sense suggest that neither the autocrat nor the democrat is more successful, but rather it is the *situation* that determines the success of a particular style. For example, when under pressure, a coach may need to be very direct and authoritarian because decisions need to be made and acted on immediately; there may be no time for consultation. At a team meeting, however, there is often much more opportunity for a coach to seek the opinions of team members.

As a guideline, business coaches are more autocratic when

- decisions are needed quickly
- team members are inexperienced or less skilled
- the team is large
- the team is accustomed to this style
- instructions have not been followed

Business coaches are more democratic when

- team members are experienced and mature
- coaching individuals or small groups
- instructions are being followed
- the team is accustomed to this style
- they see value in involving the team in decision making

An interesting study by researchers Mechikoff and Kozar[16] involved interviewing 23 coaches with good winning records. They found many different styles but four common behaviours displayed—or more specifically not displayed— by these coaches. In each case the coach did not try to enhance the performances of athletes through intimidation, deceit, embarrassment or ignoring them. These results provide excellent guidelines to be followed by the business athlete, particularly because business leadership is generally for the 'long haul' and requires the development of functional relationships with team members.

Good coaches in sport and business provide the framework or structure within which team members can thrive. For example, the coach guides the development of vision and objectives, communicates this vision and each member's responsibilities to the team, builds team culture and values, designs game plans, reviews and debriefs after performance and stimulates the development and integration of new approaches.

Business coaches recognise the need to alter their management style according to the situation in which they are coaching.

---

2. TEACHER

Successful coaches develop the knowledge and skills of team members. This point is sometimes forgotten in the hype that surrounds the so-called 'motivator' role, a stereotype for coaches in sports such as football, basketball and swimming. Similarly, in the sales field managers are often seen as motivators when in fact a more useful role is in the ongoing training and development of each member of the sales team.

For most athletes it is their coach who is the main source of information about skills which need to be developed. In industry the same can be said of most positions below professional or senior managerial level, where on-the-job training is the norm. The similarities between sport coaching and business coaching are most striking at the supervisory level where coaching is ongoing and linked very closely to the actual work role.

While sport coaches teach sport skills, they also play a major role in the development of performance attitudes. For example, ideally coaches help athletes to become self-sufficient problem solvers who can think and solve problems independently of the coach. Many of the top coaches only consider themselves successful when athletes readily make decisions about training and competition strategies for themselves. Effective coaches also look for opportunities to develop their athletes' self-confidence and concentration skills.

Business coaches are keen to develop staff members who can think on their feet and solve their own problems. A simple way this is done is by requiring staff members who seek advice to provide some alternative solutions to their own problems.

In the business athlete training we conduct in industry a central theme is the role of the manager as a business coach. Managers are trained to coach their business athletes and to help them integrate the principles of the business athlete into everyday activities.

> Business coaches develop self-reliant performers by getting them to take an active role in solving their own problems.

3. MODEL

Effective sport coaches recognise that athletes tend to imitate them. One of the reasons for this is that coaches are often called upon to demonstrate or model particular behaviours, such as how to play a backhand in squash or change a baton in a relay race. The effective coach is a role model of the temperament, self-organisation and values they desire in their athletes.

Unfortunately there are instances where coaches have operated on the 'Do as a I say, not as I do' philosophy and have set team standards—curfews, alcohol bans, no abusing referees—and then broken them. Such behaviour obviously harms trust and team harmony. In our experience, this sort of practice is much less common in sport than in business, where some executives openly do things forbidden for the rest of the staff. Simple examples of this include:

- taking leave when other staff cannot
- having separate eating areas
- precluding staff from all knowledge of senior staff meetings
- staying in unnecessarily expensive hotels
- getting performance bonuses which are not deserved.

> Good coaches give consistent messages to their team through their actions and their verbal and written communication.

4. COUNSELLOR

Some coaches have made an art form out of being gruff, menacing and totally unapproachable. Fortunately these types are now rarely seen either in sport or business, mainly because they have been shown to be ineffective in producing consistent, sustainable quality performance. There are exceptions to this, such as when a major performance turn-around is needed. Even under these conditions, however, the style will only be effective while the turn-around is occurring.

These days coaches are dealing with better educated people who expect to be kept informed. Team members want to discuss their problems more openly and coaches need basic interviewing and counselling skills if they are to be effective in dealing with issues.

Some issues which team members may want to discuss with a business coach can include:

- poor performance
- illness, stress, substance abuse
- personal problems affecting performance
- conflicts with other team members
- career decisions and opportunities
- lack of resources to do a job or poor general working conditions

In the training we conduct with coaches in sport and business, we have received very positive feedback from sessions in which basic counselling skills are introduced and practised.

> Business coaches learn and use counselling skills to deal effectively with team members on a one-to-one basis.

PERFORMANCE COMMUNICATION

Dr Mark Anshell, one of the leading international researchers and teachers of sport psychology, has identified what he has termed the 'commandments' of effective communication in sport.[17] These commandments have been modified into a list of seven **action statements** used by business coaches.

1. BE HONEST

When sport coaches are dishonest with athletes, or when business managers mislead their staff, the credibility of that person is immediately diminished. Business coaches have a high level of credibility amongst their team members, developed through being honest and direct in their communication.

2. BE OPEN

Business coaches listen to new ideas and to criticism. They don't set themselves up on a pedestal and assume that they know everything there is to know about themselves and their business.

Central to an attitude of openness are the skills of listening and questioning. In particular, business coaches actively draw out the opinions of others about issues related to the team and to their own performance.

3. BE CONSISTENT

One of the keys to managing in a competitive situation is to ensure that things are made as predictable as possible. For example, a coach preparing an athlete for a world championship will help that athlete to develop rituals which increase the predictability of their environment (eg, warm-up, mental practice, timing of meetings). In addition, the coach will try to ensure that things are done in a consistent way. A coach who is inconsistent and says one thing then does another, or fails to develop an environment that is relatively predictable, will often find performance levels falling.

4. RESPECT THE PERSON

While leading coaches criticise team members, they do this without denigrating the character of the person. Business coaches will, when necessary, point out deficiencies in a staff member's performance and look for ways to overcome these. When doing this they follow three basic principles.

- Don't attack the person's personality, that is, instead of saying 'You are lazy' , say, 'Your effort is not up to the level required'.
- Respect the person's feelings.
- End the conversation with an agreement on some positive action.

5. DON'T USE SARCASM

Sarcasm hampers communication and destroys relationships. For example, if a basketball coach tells a player, 'You move like an elephant', what are the chances of that player becoming more self-confident and open to suggestions from the coach?

Just because people laugh at a sarcastic remark does not mean that they found it funny. More than likely they are laughing to cover their embarrassment or resentment. Neither of these feelings will enhance the performance of the team member.

Business coaches avoid sarcasm and instead deal with facts and praise.

6. USE POSITIVE BODY LANGUAGE

A great deal of the information received from coaches comes from their body language. This information includes the following areas:

- posture, movement and position (facial expression, gestures, proximity)
- appearance (dress, grooming, physical condition)
- voice (tone, pitch, loudness)
- eye contact (length of gaze, direction of gaze)

The next time that you see two people talking, make a point of noting the messages they convey in these four key areas. To remember the areas, use the acronym PAVE.

7. BE A TEACHER

The teaching role of the coach has been outlined earlier. Business coaches develop clear training and development goals, provide information including modelling and allow ample time for skills to be practised.

BUSINESS COACH AFFIRMATIONS

Coaches also use positive self-statements to create the coaching style and performance they desire. The following statements are used in business athlete training programs in industry and we have included them to help you to begin integrating the concepts from this chapter into your daily rituals. Use them regularly if your role involves coaching.

- 'I am an effective leader.'
- 'I teach skills and assist my team members to become better performers in all areas of their lives.'
- 'I am a role model for my team members.'
- 'I use counselling skills when assisting my staff to deal with problems.'
- 'I assist team members who become increasingly more self-reliant and confident.'
- 'I am open, honest and consistent in my dealings with team members.'
- 'I respect my team members as people who make a positive contribution to the performance of the team.'

14

SUMMARY

Athletes in sport and business continually meet and interact with people from all walks of life. Those people fall into three general groups, and the success of individuals, teams, organisations and countries depends upon how they deal with the people in each group.

In the first group are those people who want to see athletes succeeding and winning. We believe that it is important for business athletes to be members of this group. This means encouraging other athletes to be the best that they can be, and taking pleasure from seeing the success of others.

In the second group are those people who take little interest in whether athletes succeed or fail. On occasion this group can be mobilised to support a sporting hero; however, it is rare for them to acknowledge business athletes. This group has the potential to be educated, enthused and involved, and one of the important roles of the business athlete is to do exactly this.

In the final group are the people who 'knock' the winners. They dislike athletes who, in their eyes, are too successful. Unfortunately, this group has been too influential in shaping the community's attitude to success.

Business athletes accept that committing themselves and their organisation to being the best that they can be will inevitably attract the attention of some members of the final group. Instead of taking it personally, business athletes choose not to let these people affect their motivation. They realise that these people often act this way out of unhappiness or feelings of inadequacy. When the opportunity presents itself, business athletes find ways to make these people feel better about themselves and to succeed in their own lives.

Business athletes are team members. Our hope is that this

book and the training program from which it has been developed will help to improve our community's overall attitude towards success. We need a community which wants everyone to succeed and which lifts up our heroes and encourages others to follow their example. Australia has many resources but none more important than our business athletes, who train and compete and win on the playing fields of the world.

The challenge is there for you to be a business athlete in your chosen field and to be a part of our national business athlete team.

Play well.

ENDNOTES

1. Locke EA & Latham GP, *Goal setting. A motivational technique that works*, Englewood Cliffs, New Jersey, Prentice-Hall, 1984.
2. Holmes à Court R, in De Bono, E, *Tactics*, Fontana, Great Britain, 1985, p. 103.
3. The Government of Singapore, *Singapore The Next Lap*, Times Editions, Singapore 1991, p. 57.
4. Cerutty PW, *Athletics. How to become a champion*, Stanley Paul, London, 1960, p. 78.
5. Thompson D, in Gelman S (Ed), *Official Olympic Souvenir Program; Games of the xxiiird olympiad Los Angeles 1984*, Australian Consolidated Press, Sydney, 1984, p. 71.
6. Bertrand J, *Born to win*, Corgi & Bantam Australia, Sydney, 1985, p. 352.
7. Peters TJ & Waterman RH, *In search of excellence*, Harper & Row, New York, 1982.
8. Mansell N in Loehr Dr JE, *Mental toughness training for sports*, Stephen Greene Press, Massachusetts, 1986.
9. Mansell N, reported in the *Advertiser* newspaper, October 31, 1991.
10. Schulz JH & Luthe W, *Autogenic methods*, Grune & Stratton, New York, 1969.
11. Flintoff D, reported on *'A Current Affair'*, The Nine Network, Australia, 1991.
12. Burton D, 'Winning isn't everything: Examining the impact of performance goals on collegiate swimmers' cognitions and performance'; *The Sport Psychologist*, 3, 1989, pp 105–132.
13. Winter GJ & Martin CA, *SASI PSYCH Basic Training Program* (second edition), South Australian Sports Institute, 1991.
14. Martens R, *Imagery in sport*, Paper presented at the Medical

and Scientific Aspects of Elitism in Sport Conference, Brisbane, Australia, 1982.

15. Martens R, *Coaches' guide to sport psychology*, Human Kinetics Publishers, Illinois, 1987, p. 13.
16. Mechkoff & Kozar in Anshell M, *Sport Psychology; From theory to practice*, Gorsuch Scarisbrick Publishers, Arizona, 1990.
17. Anshell M, *Sport Psychology; From theory to practice*, Gorsuch Scarisbrick Publishers, Arizona, 1990.

HAMILTON WINTER INTERNATIONAL

Hamilton Winter International is a consultancy that offers individuals and organisations systematic training and development using the processes derived from *The Business Athlete*.

The consultancy can provide

- One-day training seminars
- Half-day training seminars
- Personalised management coaching
- Inhouse conferences
- Residential conferences

Through its national links the company provides qualified and licensed business athlete trainers who are able to provide full company installations of *The Business Athlete* program as well as work with divisions, teams and individuals when particular skills, attitude and knowledge development are required.

The Business Athlete training program is modular in form and, after a specific training analysis, is tailored carefully to achieve the most appropriate outcomes for participants.

Our consultants are also available for speaking engagements.

For further information about the company's consulting services contact us at the following numbers:

Sydney	(02) 956 8100
Melbourne	(03) 820 2477
Adelaide	(08) 373 1751
Perth	(09) 481 2390
Brisbane	(07) 870 5046